A Sea of Troubles

Pairing Literary and Informational Texts to Address Social Inequality

Elizabeth James
B. H. James

ROWMAN & LITTLEFIELD
Lanham • Boulder • New York • London

Published by Rowman & Littlefield
An imprint of The Rowman & Littlefield Publishing Group, Inc.
4501 Forbes Boulevard, Suite 200, Lanham, Maryland 20706
www.rowman.com

6 Tinworth Street, London SE11 5AL, United Kingdom

British Library Cataloguing in Publication Information Available

Library of Congress Cataloging-in-Publication Data

Names: James, Elizabeth, 1984– author. | James, B. H., 1978- author.
Title: A sea of troubles : pairing literary and informational texts to address social
    inequality / Elizabeth James, B. H. James.
Description: Lanham : Rowman & Littlefield, [2021] | Includes bibliographical
    references and index. | Summary: "Sea of Troubles shows teachers how literature
    and informational texts can work together to enhance each other and, by extension,
    enhance students' abilities to critically think and respond to the sea of troubles that
    pervades society"—Provided by publisher.
Identifiers: LCCN 2020048548 (print) | LCCN 2020048549 (ebook) |
    ISBN 9781475857504 (cloth) | ISBN 9781475857511 (paperback) |
    ISBN 9781475857528 (epub)
Subjects: LCSH: American literature—Study and teaching. | English Literature—Study
    and teaching. | Social problems in literature. | Social justice in literature. | Other
    (Philosophy) in literature.
Classification: LCC PS41 .J36 2021 (print) | LCC PS41 (ebook) | DDC 810.71—dc23
LC record available at https://lccn.loc.gov/2020048548
LC ebook record available at https://lccn.loc.gov/2020048549

∞™ The paper used in this publication meets the minimum requirements of American National Standard for Information Sciences—Permanence of Paper for Printed Library Materials, ANSI/NISO Z39.48-1992.

A Sea of Troubles

Contents

Preface

In mid-February of 2020, we facilitated a workshop at the California Association of Teachers of English (CATE) Conference. The workshop was titled *A Sea of Troubles: Investigating Otherness and Social Injustice with Originally Paired Texts.*

The concept behind the presentation was based on that of this book, which at the time of the conference we had begun writing.

We began the presentation by asking the teachers in the room to make a list—not a list of books or a list of teaching strategies, but a list of issues and concepts and things they found important enough to discuss in the classroom. In other words, we asked them to name the waves in our current world's "sea of troubles."

The group came up with the following list:

- Gun violence
- Fake news
- Police brutality
- Polarized politics
- Achievement gap
- Totalitarianism
- Reproductive rights
- Mental health
- Addiction
- Financial inequality
- "Me, too"
- Immigration
- Access to resources

- Climate change
- Bullying
- Homelessness
- Detention centers
- Unity and variety
- Coronavirus
- What is truth?
- Racial inequality
- Microaggression
- State Surveillance (Big Brother)
- LGBTQ rights/inequality
- Issue fatigue

From there, we asked the teachers in the room to huddle up and choose one issue in particular—just one—and work with the teachers around them to create a list of books that deal with that issue. We then shared out the results. Here are two such lists:

Racial Inequality
- *To Kill a Mockingbird* by Harper Lee
- *The Tragedy of Othello* by William Shakespeare
- *Of Mice and Men* by John Steinbeck
- *The Bluest Eye* by Toni Morrison
- *Notes of a Native Son* by James Baldwin
- *I Know Why the Caged Bird Sings* by Maya Angelou
- *Born a Crime* by Trevor Noah
- *The Hate U Give* by Angie Thomas
- *Underground Railroad* by Colson Whitehead
- *Heart of Darkness* by Joseph Conrad
- *The Brief Wondrous Life of Oscar Wao* by Junot Díaz

LGBTQ Rights/Inequality
- *Aristotle and Dante Discover the History of the Universe* by Benjamin Alire Sáenz
- *The Perks of Being a Wallflower* by Stephen Chbosky
- Multiple plays by William Shakespeare (*The Merchant of Venice*, for instance)
- *The Laramie Project* by Moisés Kaufman and Stephen Belber
- *Angels in America* by Tony Kushner
- *I Wish You All the Best* by Mason Deaver
- *Gross Indecency* by Moisés Kaufman
- *The Picture of Dorian Gray* by Oscar Wilde
- *Symptoms of Being Human* by Jeff Garvin

This exercise helped teachers recognize (or remember) that plays and novels and poetry hold up a mirror to our world and can be a tool for helping our students not only improve their reading and writing skills but also understand and participate more deeply in the world in which they live.

THE PURPOSE OF THIS BOOK

As the lists above demonstrate, these are troubling times. It would probably be hubris on our part to believe that people at other points in history did not think the same of their times. Yet: we, and the students we teach, are up against "a sea of troubles."

The lists also demonstrate that, when it comes to using literature to explore contemporary real-world issues, there is no shortage of works with which to do that. In this book, we will model units centered on ten works that are likely to be sitting in your school's bookroom. This, of course, does not mean that you *must* choose those books in order to apply the strategies to follow. Rather, these strategies and activities can be adapted and applied to the literature of your choice.

The specific image of a *sea of troubles*, from Shakespeare's most famous speech, still resonates today. Scrolling on one's phone, absorbing the injustice and calamity around us, can feel isolating and overwhelming. What is the individual to do? How do we not get dragged under?

So, the question is, as English teachers, do we simply suffer those troubles and carry on as usual, or do we, within the context of the work of an English course, take arms? English teachers have always known that teaching themes and universality is part of their work. But what if we could take it further? What if we could use the texts in book rooms across America and reimagine an English classroom that very purposefully tied beautiful, compelling literary arts with the real world around us, pairing those literary texts with informative nonfiction that could enhance our understanding of those texts *and* of our current besieged world?

A Sea of Troubles will provide strategies for engaging with challenging social issues through the rigorous study of literature. By focusing on the global and timeless themes of social injustice (specifically through the lens of "Otherness"), students will be able to humanize the problems they see around them.

The book will also model how pairing literary and informational texts will aid student engagement with these issues. We will show you how you can pair seemingly disparate literature together to examine timeless issues, as well as how to embed opportunities to investigate informational texts in a meaningful and symbiotic fashion, so that students recognize how fiction reflects the world, and the world is reflected in fiction.

LITERARY VERSUS INFORMATIONAL TEXTS

The Common Core standards, currently adopted in forty-one states, differentiate between two types of reading: literary and informational. In fact, the Common Core established guidelines for the teaching of these two forms, such that, at the high school level, students should be reading 70 percent informational texts and 30 percent literature. These guidelines led to a perception (now known to be a misperception) that Common Core called for less literature. This misperception was based upon the misunderstanding that the above percentages were in reference to reading in the English classroom. The percentages, however, were in reference to the entirety of a student's reading (across all disciplines—history, math, science, etc.).

Therefore, given the new guidelines, students should be reading just as much (if not more) fiction, poetry, and drama in their English classes. And the authors of the standards released a statement to that effect.

Nevertheless, since the incarnation of the Common Core, there has been a tug-of-war between districts and teachers about the need to incorporate more nonfiction texts into classrooms. And a lot of that tug-of-war seems to come from the fact that nonfiction and informational texts are easier to assess on standardized testing and therefore appear more often on such tests, thereby naturally leading to school leaders calling for that difference in quantity to be reflected in instruction.

It isn't a bad point. We live in a world in which there is a never-ceasing deluge of information, and so much of it is so important. It is easy to tune out. Additionally, we know that our present is a time when quality information matters more than it ever has. We need to be able to discern when we are receiving half the story. So, in theory, an increase in nonfiction, informational reading makes sense.

But just as we would argue (and the framers of the Common Core would argue) that students should be reading high-quality works in fiction, drama, and poetry, so too should the nonfiction texts that are chosen for students be of high quality. It is irresponsible to merely increase one and two-page excerpts from informational texts that have next to nothing to do with anything else students are learning about. That is teaching to the test to the detriment of the students and their education.

Substandard informational texts do not increase a student's ability to read and write. They become, in short, a series of unconnected and meaningless tasks, perpetuating the narrative for the student that reading and writing are unimportant and do not matter to them.

LITERARY PLUS INFORMATIONAL TEXTS

However, when literary and informational texts are paired in the context of a unit that engages meaningfully with a universal concept or a social issue, learning becomes more authentic and more relevant to our students. In such a case, informational texts serve the purpose of introducing students to the real-life issues that need addressing, but the role of fiction (and drama, and poetry) is to make those issues human.

At the heart of every issue are the humans who face it, and it is through imaginative literature that we can interact with, engage with, and, as Scout Finch does, walk in the shoes of people—like us, but unlike us—struggling against conflicts that still plague our society. And the strategic and meaningful pairing of informational and literary texts will equip today's students to "take arms against" that "sea of troubles" and, hopefully, finally, "end them."

AND, FINALLY

During the time we wrote this text, the news domestically and internationally was changing at lightning speed. We wrote during the COVID-19 isolation, the demonstrations in response to George Floyd's death, and more. It is our sincere hope that teachers reading this book will continue to show, in real-time, how injustice and inequality are shaping our families, our communities, and our nation. Please read this book and consider the world around you—what stories are coming to light on a daily basis—to aid you in pairing iconic literature with its real-time reflections all around us.

Acknowledgments

We would like to dedicate this book to our little boys, Tom and Sam, who we think are just the best. We love you so much.

Thank you to Rowman and Littlefield, in particular our editors, Tom Koerner and Carlie Wall, for their guidance throughout this process.

Thank you also to our past students—Kyla Figueroa, Lizette Orozco, Kirsten Basilio, and Lindsey Shobert—whose essays appear as samples in this book.

And to *all* of our students: past, present, and future. You always have been and always will be worth all of the hard work. Keep reading and thinking and figuring it all out. The world needs you.

Introduction

OTHERNESS IN THE CLASSROOM, IN THE WORLD, AND IN LITERATURE

Many of the issues in our "sea of troubles" have a common concept at their core: Otherness. Therefore, the chapters that follow, while each addressing a more specific issue, will also explore the causes and consequences of Otherness.

Furthermore, an exploration of Otherness will inevitably bring to light a series of related concepts, all of which our chapters, in various ways, will introduce and begin to investigate:

- Identity
- Tribalism
- Alienation
- Dehumanization

Perhaps most importantly in the context of English Language Arts, the following chapters will explore the extent to which Otherness is supported—or created—by *language*.

Otherness is a concept rarely taught in literature classes until the university level. And yet, it is pivotal for understanding the "why" and "so what" questions that compel us to study great works of literature. Our twenty-first-century students understand the stakes of identity politics. They live in a curated world of their own making, inhabiting a duality of self never before seen in the world. Who they are and who they purport to be do not always match.

In her 2017 book *The Origin of Others*, based on her Charles Eliot Norton Lectures at Harvard University, Toni Morrison states that "Because there are such major benefits in creating and sustaining an Other, it is important to (1) identify the benefits and (2) discover what may be the social/political results of repudiating those benefits."[1] As Morrison suggests, students should be encouraged to question the power structure behind Otherness. Who benefits from "creating and sustaining" the perception of Otherness, and how can those motives and benefits, and thereby that perception, be called into question?

Morrison also questions the inherent need for an Other and the concept's persistence in society:

> *What is the nature of Othering's comfort, its allure, its power (social, psychological, or economical)? Is it the thrill of belonging—which implies being part of something bigger than one's solo self, and therefore stronger? My initial view leans toward the social/psychological need for a 'stranger,' an Other in order to define the estranged self (the crowd seeker is always the lonely one).*

There is something so human in creating and passing on a story of exclusion—particularly when one recognizes Otherness is something we all at one time or another will feel, and, equally true, something we will all, at one time or another, participate in ourselves.

Otherness is in so many ways necessary to life. Evolutionarily, it made sense for survival to know to which group you belonged, and to which you did not. Space and safety were gained and understood based on who identified as what. This tribalism was not only related to safety; we learn, in part, who we are by who we are *not*.

This is important information because, though our identities are formed early on, we must be able to recognize the extent to which our identities are, to varying degrees, are the result of a series of choices about us that we did not participate in. We inherit large portions of our identities. And with this recognition, we must be willing to move away from exclusionary thoughts and beliefs, and move toward a pattern of behavior that is purposefully and mindfully more inclusive.

OTHERNESS IN OUR STUDENTS' DAILY LIVES

Activity One: Examining our In-Group

When first introducing these new concepts, spend a little time talking about the paradigm of Otherness and tribalism. Try to get students thinking about what they do or do not know about themselves, and how they got that certainty. In other words, what lessons for each of our communities was explicitly or implicitly taught to us? What "team" were we brought up to know we were on? To help students out, give them some topics to think of. What was explicitly or implicitly messaged to them about what was or was not acceptable about each of the following:

- Politics?
- Religion?
- Race?
- Sexuality?
- Class?
- Culture?
- Gender?

Have them write about this experience for a few minutes. Is this a part of their identity they feel they formed themselves, or is this a part of their identity they inherited from their family? What was the cost of this lesson? What were the benefits? If they themselves become parents, are there concepts or values they will want to instill in their children—frontloading the next generation's identity so it aligns with their own, or do they see a problem with that construct? Has this inherited tribalism led to the improvement of the community, or has it created division?

Collect the documents and keep them away from students as they discover the costs and benefits of tribalism within the literature and informational texts they are studying. At the end of the unit, return the students' initial reflections. Give them time to brainstorm over which major characters benefited from the process of tribalism and Otherness, and who suffered for it. Have them think about what the respective author is suggesting about identity politics. If a society understands itself by knowing what it is not, how is the society strengthened or weakened? And how is humanity strengthened or weakened?

Activity Two: Demonstrating the Other

Students may quickly come to analyze the costs and benefits of Othering and identity politics as it applies to characters in oft-studied texts. But that does not necessarily mean they will transfer those lessons to their own lives. After all, it is always much easier to see what other people are doing wrong, rather than to see our own mistakes and missteps.

In order to bring the lesson of universal Othering home to your students, simply ask them to journal for three minutes or so about a time they knew they were being excluded from something—it could be a conversation, a clique, a party, an opportunity. Challenge them to write it in the present tense, as if it is happening right now to them all over again, and challenge them to write how it feels.

Take a moment to share out (if they are comfortable) or share one yourself. Then have students write about a time when they Othered another—when they implicitly or explicitly, passively or actively participated in the exclusion of someone else. Again, have them write it in the present tense. Was it easier just to stay quiet? Was it not a big deal at the time? Did they gain or lose credibility with others by excluding someone?

Ask your students how many of them had a story to write for the first prompt. Probably everyone will raise their hand. By being alive and in social settings, everyone has felt this way, and though we get better at recognizing it and dealing with it, being Othered is a thing that does not seem to stop. Then ask your students who has Othered another. Probably everyone raises their hand again.

At this point, facilitate a conversation about how that can be possible. How can we journal about the pain it causes us, and then—oftentimes thoughtlessly, purposelessly, and, worst, without really noticing we're doing it—do it to others? Why is the pain we feel when it is *us* not enough to make us remember and resist inflicting that pain on others?

OTHERNESS IN LITERATURE

When we begin to apply the universal concept of Otherness to literature, we find that a story that is anchored on the exploration of the Other in society is a story with built-in conflict and drama. This can be an individual that doesn't fit into society (your Boo Radleys) or it could be a person or people that are in a hierarchy within their story and do not hold the power of the infrastructure they are in (your Calibans or Shylocks).

If students are struggling with the literary component, try a brief ten-minute story time. Read Dr. Seuss's *The Sneetches*[2] aloud to the group (when all else fails, always turn to children's literature for a simple, accessible demonstration of a troublesome topic). It is the story of haves and have-nots, all on the basis of what one group looks like. It is, in short, a way to introduce the concept of prejudice. Have the students graph out the book for conflict and resolution and *power* or status. Who has it, who wants it, and how is that central to understanding the text? If they can do that, they can understand Shakespeare's *The Merchant of Venice*.

The good(ish) news is there is never a story without conflict, and so a story based around Otherness is already off to a rocking good start. Not all stories rely on this concept to create conflict—for instance, Hamlet does not

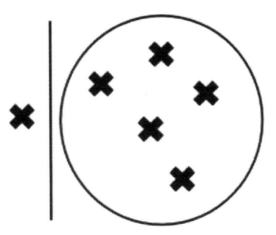

Figure 0.1   The Other in Literature.

experience Otherness in his existential crisis of a play. But Otherness remains an important concept to our understanding of literature. What does it mean to belong? And to what extent does that belonging enable the exclusion of others? And why are we okay with this?

Figure 0.1 demonstrates the story of the Other in literature. The circle represents those that are "in." They have access to whatever it is that's worth having access to. Old Money in *The Great Gatsby,* for instance, would be represented by those X's in the circle. Gatsby, with his absurd attempts at being equal with such grandiosity, is the X that is denied entry to the circle.

By examining the above diagram, students will come to recognize that the point of view of someone who is already "in" is not necessarily an interesting place from which to tell a story. Who cares about a person who has already gained (or inherited) access to a society of their choosing? What is far more compelling, far more relatable and dynamic, is the story of the person who can see the party but knows they are not invited.

This is the character that is considered "Other" in literature, and they are often the most memorable characters—Gatsby, Shylock, Boo Radley, Tom Robinson, Huck, and Jim—united not only by their Otherness but by the injustice of their exclusion. So why, as Morrison suggests, is (or, perhaps, has there been) such a benefit to naming who among us is "the stranger"?

This is the ultimate question of this book. How do we change this particular pattern? How do we outgrow this awful tendency we have to Other one another? We cannot yet offer a concrete path, but it is our sincere hope that by employing this philosophy of investigating the cost of Otherness in our classrooms, our students will find a way—finally—forward.

NOTES

1. Toni Morrison, *The Origin of Others* (Cambridge, MA: Harvard University Press, 2017).

2. Dr. Seuss, "The Sneetches," in *The Sneetches and Other Stories* (London: HarperCollins Publishers Children's Books, 2017).

Chapter 1

Syntactical Othering and
The Merchant of Venice

Choosing which Shakespeare play to tackle in a classroom can be a hot-button issue among English teachers. This chapter will suggest a less common choice: *The Merchant of Venice.* In this chapter, we'll see how choosing a problematic text can be an avenue into talking about ongoing problems within society. What were we doing then, and why? And what are we (still) doing now, and why? Why are there some patterns society just can't seem to break?

The activities in this chapter are more reflective in nature; by beginning with some close-reading activities (of scenes, of character arcs, of patterns) students will enhance their ability to recognize and discuss how Othering manifests in a text. This skill will inevitably bear fruit with later units, and it is worth providing some fundamental practice early on.

There are certainly additional opportunities for incorporating nonfiction and informational texts into this unit. For instance, merely pulling Lit Crit on either Shylock or Portia from fifty to a hundred years ago can really open students' eyes to how readers have struggled and, perhaps, misunderstood these two characters for generations.

However, the majority of this chapter will demonstrate how you can simultaneously discuss a societal issue of injustice while keeping your focus directly on the play. Rigorous examination of pacing and characterization and imagery do not need to pause in order to investigate how language props up the myth of the Other.

DID SHAKESPEARE JUST DO THAT?
DID HE MEAN TO DO THAT?

The more we consider this particular play, the more shockingly subversive we find it to be. The play was produced and marketed as a comedy for hundreds of years, with no questions asked. That history is accurate. However, the diction of the play, the characterization of our players, and the odd resolution all stand on the page today as they did in the 1600s. And what is on the page does not read as funny.

It is as if the biggest joke of the play is on us: to witness how easily an audience will believe who is "good" and who is "bad" if it matches our own expectations—even when the textual evidence counteracts that expectation. The play is a manifesto about the dangers of Otherness in society—in any society. We see what we want to see. We believe whom we want to believe. And we laugh at whom society says we can laugh at.

The problem with teaching *The Merchant of Venice* is it is still regarded as the Shakespeare play wherein a heroine really shines. Portia of Belmont is still, by overwhelming margins, supposed to personify righteousness and wit, which she does. But, upon closer examination, she also personifies the danger of tribalism and living in a world that demands an Other.

What is brilliant about the play is, in part, how both societal groups (the Jewish group, personified by Shylock, and the Christians, by, well, everyone else) ignore the humanity of the opposing side. This basic inability to grant dignity to others makes it incredibly difficult finding "good guys" and "bad guys" in this play. Everyone is stubborn. Everyone is blind to their own misdeeds.

Now, for our purposes, this is an essential point of the text. There are a million moments where any number of characters could hit the brakes and be more constructive and avoid, for instance, having their guts cut out. But no one seems to be able to see how, as they continue to participate in Othering, they worsen Othering—even for themselves.

For instance, though Shylock is now often read (at the least) as the most compelling character in the play, he simply can't be our hero, because he believes the answer to his wrongs is to wrong in turn. He believes murder will empower him, and that is a base idea, unworthy of a mind such as his. His treatment as an Other and for being Othered has resulted in a loss of personhood himself. He shows no curiosity, no concern for any of the Christians in the courtroom; he is monomaniacal, and that is his tragic flaw—he cannot extend the human compassion that he himself was denied.

Similarly, the Christians in the play—personified mostly by Antonio and Portia—fail to ever grasp (let alone try to grasp) how their behavior has brought about a focused and bloodthirsty lust for vengeance. In the courtroom, with death but moments away, Antonio begs his friends not to bother reasoning with Shylock's "Jewish heart."[1] Language such as this demonstrates a lack of human understanding of the pain Antonio himself has brought down on his own head. As the saying goes, he made his bed when he treated Shylock so abhorrently, but he fails to see the connection between his actions and the bed of death in which Shylock now wants him to lie.

Because he doesn't see Shylock as fully human, he cannot believe in Shylock's pain.

Because neither group understands their misbehavior, neither group can claim victory. It is this that makes the play so unsatisfying to a modern audience. If the curtain rose on the next morning in Venice, nothing has changed. No lessons have been learned. Otherness and tribalism will still rule the day, and the bloody pattern will repeat.

Activity One: The Dangers of Otherness

If it will feed nothing else, it will feed my revenge.[2]

The Merchant of Venice is a play that is remarkably savvy (and underrated) in its ability to demonstrate the human cost of Otherness and tribalism in a society. When we exert our own viewpoint over that of someone around us, we, either passively or actively, choose ourselves above others. When we recognize we are within a group of safety and camaraderie, it implicitly acknowledges that there are those among us who are not. Our safety and belonging can sometimes only exist when others are denied that same comfort. And therein lies the danger. What do we risk by feeling we've gained? What does Othering do to a society?

This play is, of course, anchored on the Christians whose identity relies in part on recognizing their differences from the Jews. Theological differences are never hashed out, just communities co-existing in a detrimental way. It doesn't matter whether or not Antonio is a "good" Christian or a "bad" Christian—he is Christian; therefore, he is unlike Shylock. His identity as a Christian means he is allowed to spit on and mistreat Shylock, and expect no recourse.

So before we jump into a play where Christians have the privilege of being who or what they wish to be, while always remaining Christian—whereas Shylock is never allowed to be anything other than a Jew—we must consider how each character's individual identity determines their actions.

From whence does this identity come? Is it natural to them, or circumstantial? Is it determinative to their particular character's resolution, or was it malleable? What was gained and lost by these shifts in identity?

Have students keep track of each of the following character's shifts in identity:

- Portia
- Bassanio
- Antonio
- Shylock
- Jessica
- Launcelot

Let them see how the inherited identity of Jewishness drives Jessica away from her father's home, for instance. Her identity is solely being part of the Jewish community and she can't be seen as anything else until she converts to Christianity. Shedding her religious identity allows her access to idyllic Belmont; a place she would not be allowed to occupy otherwise.

It begs the question: is it worth it? What is the implicit or explicit cost of clinging to or surrendering our identities? How can something so important be so problematic?

Additionally, consider having students view Heather C. McGhee's TED Talk entitled "Racism Has a Cost for Everyone."[3] This video details how the identity issues between Antonio and Shylock (and others in the play as well) are still functioning in full force today, and how detrimental these issues are for all of us. As McGhee puts it, questions of identity cannot be "zero sum." Students can view the TED talk for themes that compare and contrast with that of the play, or write a reflection about how the two texts seem to be speaking to each other.

WHEN THE BAD GUYS SEEM GOOD, WHEN THE GOOD GUYS SEEM BAD

Activity Two: Whom Are We Supposed to Be Rooting For?

I am not bound to please thee with my answers.[4]

Consider starting your unit by having a story time. Have the students listen to the plot, as you tell it, before they read it. It may go something like this:

"*The Merchant of Venice* is a play with two simultaneous plots. There is a rich merchant named Antonio, who has money to spend. His best friend, Bassanio, asks for a loan so he can court a rich lady named Portia. Antonio doesn't have the cash available because his ships are all out to sea, so they go to a Jewish moneylender named Shylock for the cash. Instead of interest, Shylock, who hates Antonio, writes a contract that says if Antonio can't pay, Shylock gets to cut a pound of flesh from Antonio's body.

"The second plot is about Portia, the rich lady Bassanio wants to marry. She isn't allowed to pick her own husband, because her father, as his dying wish, created a test wherein strangers come and answer riddles in order to marry her.

Portia is incredibly smart, and this is frustrating. Portia and Bassanio marry, but Bassanio is called away to support Antonio, who has broken his contract with Shylock, and is set to die. Portia disguises herself as a lawyer, infiltrates the court, and saves Antonio by stopping Shylock collecting his pound of flesh."

After a summary like that, have students write one simple sentence stating who the protagonist is in the play, and whom they assume the antagonist is going to be. If the summary is all they have to work with, they will probably suggest Shylock is the antagonist, and Portia is the protagonist, right?

But it's just not that simple in this play. People and their identities as "good" or "bad" are not what they seem. Because of syntactical Othering, people are often empowered by their "in group" to declare what is good or bad, right or wrong, just or unjust, but saying it doesn't make it so.

Merchant is a story in which both our main characters, Shylock and Portia, are outside looking in, and, as discussed in the Introduction, this conflict is inherently dramatic because it immediately creates sympathy within the audience. Because we have all universally experienced it, we can all universally sympathize with those enduring it.

Fascinatingly, you could make a case for either Shylock or Portia being the most "Othered" character in the play. Shylock is, of course, Jewish, and, as such, is persecuted and degraded by the Christians in the play, namely Antonio, the titled merchant, who, among other things, spits on him and calls him a dog. This ethnic Otherness means that Shylock cannot work in the same businesses as Christians, can't live among Christians, and cannot receive the same justice or mercy that Christians in the play can.

Indeed, this prevention of his human rights and dignity make him a fine candidate for being considered the protagonist of this play. And yet. Shylock is not the titled character, he is not in most scenes, and his beef with Antonio provides a climax for the play, but an unsatisfying one. And you can't really have a protagonist who is not part of the resolution. Indeed, as soon as Shylock says "I am content"[5] no one mentions him again, as if he were a bad dream.

Our second contender for the Othered protagonist is Portia. When we first meet Portia she is being ruled by her dead father—the motif of overbearing (and thwarted) fathers runs across all women in the play. She is beautiful and smart and witty, and yet, though she is the sole heir of Belmont, she cannot rule the roost as she sees fit because her patriarchal society has enabled her dead father to control her postmortem in an inane test that is unworthy of her wit. Portia is a character we come to understand as being Othered from society because of her sex. She cannot gain access to the world of learned wits until she is freed into marriage—an odd narrative choice.

So, if we understand the definition of a protagonist to be the main character who changes over the course of a story, who here deserves that title? How can we have a comedy/drama where we don't even know who the main character is? Honestly, would anyone bother saying it is Antonio, the actual merchant of Venice?

Have the students engage in a debate on this point: Who is the protagonist, and who is the antagonist, and how do we know? Students can choose sides, or you can choose for them, but they should be prepared to debate their peers armed with textual evidence and analysis to support their claims.

After the class wrestles with this question, have students respond independently to a simple writing prompt: Why on earth would Shakespeare choose to make this question so opaque? What purpose does it serve in the text?

Though answers will vary, hopefully students will arrive at something like this: even though they are fighting each other and hurting each other and dehumanizing each other, they have more in common than not.

Activity Three: That Stupid Casket Test— Symbolism, or a Nasty Trick?

All that glitters is not gold;
Often have you heard that told:
Many a man his life hath sold
But my outside to behold:
Gilded tombs do worms enfold.[6]

Of course, the central Otherness of the play is personified in the courtroom scene. There, "The Jew," as everyone calls him, is finally going to receive the same justice under the law that Christians would. It is here that the mere proposal of equality is destroyed, and it is here that Shylock is destroyed because of his Otherness for sport (just ask the jeering Gratiano, who voices the cruel love of destruction of the Other, Shylock). But laughing at something Other is introduced much earlier.

After reading the casket test scenes, stop for a Socratic Seminar. What is the point of those scenes? What do they symbolize? What do they foreshadow? And what are they doing there? It will be interesting to see what student's make of these seemingly disconnected (and dragging) scenes without any additional guidance.

After students wrestle with the purpose of the casket test, consider an alternative, more subversive reason for this subplot.

The stupid casket test is designed by Portia's father as a test of character for suitors of his daughter. The idea is simply this: a good man will know that treasure is not always about the most gilded opportunity. Now, obviously we know this is not foolproof, because the fool Bassanio figures it out. We know he pursues Portia because she "is richly left" not because he loves her, and we know he asks to be costumed to look more gilded himself, thereby gaining access to the test for Portia to begin with.

The irony of Bassanio picking the iron casket when he himself knows the thinness of appearance, and then gaining Portia (and her fortune) proves that the test (from this source of patriarchal postmortem power) is flawed and silly. The real stakes of the play have not yet been introduced.

These dragging scenes are designed to make the audience laugh—and laugh we do, as the Prince of Morocco and the Spaniard are ridiculous, self-involved clowns. These scenes are often played with over-the-top clowning, and that's a necessary choice, because there's nothing that funny about the text. People who look different from the golden Portia want to marry her—but Otherness is introduced as naturally revolting, and Portia is "saved" by them with the introduction of Bassanio on the scene.

But notice that these scenes are absolutely untethered to the plot of the play, and unnecessary. Howsoever, what they manage to do is introduce *Otherness as comedy*. The audience becomes complicit in laughing at the ludicrousness of a Black man and a Spaniard having gall enough to try to marry Portia.

It may be designed for cheap laughs, or it may be designed to implicate the audience in what is later done to Shylock. Modern audiences can't laugh at that courtroom scene. It's dark and scary and troublesome. But just as we had no problem laughing at the dumb casket test when we knew the lover Bassanio was on his way to choose right, Gratiano has no problem laughing at Shylock as he is destroyed and as Portia is on her way to setting society's hierarchy of power back up right again. Perhaps Shakespeare caters to these earlier cheap laughs in order to demonstrate everyone's complicity in Othering others for our amusement—a dark suggestion, indeed.

Have students choose one instance of subversiveness they see in the play, and discuss its impact on our understanding of it. This is a great opportunity for original analysis and provides a chance to explore multiple readings of the text. Here are a few topic ideas:

1. How does Shakespeare subvert ideas about traditional gender roles in the text?
2. How does Shakespeare subvert ideas about protagonists and antagonists?
3. How does Shakespeare culturally subvert ideas about Christian superiority?
4. How does the play subvert expectations of comedy?
5. How does the play subvert cultural expectations of the Jew archetype at the time?

How is Shakespeare subverting the audience's predetermined expectations? And what does this subversion suggest?

Students could work in small groups to prepare presentations on the above topics (or others), and then could share out with the whole group a presentation focused on two things:

1. How that particular topic demonstrates subversion, and
2. Why they think Shakespeare wanted to subvert these expectations.

MONKEYS AND MARRIAGE, RINGS AND REGRETS

Activity Four: A Play in which the Enemy Seems Kind of Right

The villainy you teach me, I will execute, and it shall go hard but I will better the instruction.[7]

At the end of Act IV, Shylock disappears, never to be mentioned again. At this point in the unit, have students write a letter to Shylock. What do they think of him? His motivations? His fixation on Antonio? Do they believe in his Act IV resolution? Do they, perhaps, sympathize with him? What can we infer about this play that creates sympathy with the only would-be murderer on stage?

The Merchant of Venice is now considered by critics a "problem play"— in short, a play that defies the characteristics of any particular set of genre criteria. And this is true. Consider the list of characteristics necessary for a Shakespeare play to be considered a comedy:

1. Cross-dressing and/or disguise
2. Women in power within the text
3. Bawdy humor
4. Ends with a wedding and a bedding

Based on these criteria, *Merchant* is a straight Shakespearean comedy—no question! It checks each of the above boxes. And yet. Since World War II it has been absolutely impossible for audiences not to be troubled by Shylock and his plight; it's hard to laugh if your comic heroes are getting what they want at the expense of someone whom society has degraded and exiled.

And it's hard to have an antagonist at the center of a comedy that we feel so bad for. He's just too human a character. His language, his power, his motivations surpass all societal prejudices. We can't help but be compelled by him.

Now we all know Shakespeare freely lifted, repackaged, and regifted other people's plots all the time. *Romeo and Juliet* was lifted from an old poem, Romeus and Juliet, for instance. He didn't even try that hard to hide the lifting. His gift, of course, is to take someone else's proposal, plot, or protagonist, and reimagine them into three-dimensional existence—to give them a depth and humanity they lacked before. This gift is why we study Shakespeare and not Ben Jonson or Christopher Marlowe in schools across the world.

Speaking of Marlowe—he had a play called *The Jew of Malta* starring Barabas, an evil Jewish character that was murderous and despised. The play was a hit, and the idea gave Shakespeare an idea. What if he absconded with the familiar British trope of an evil Jewish clown figure, and presented him *as* that same clown, put him in a comedy, but allowed his words to tell a different story entirely? Barabas is a Jew in Italy who has a problem with Christian hypocrisy, but he himself is a clear, bloodthirsty villain. He says things like, *"As for myself, I walk abroad a-nights / And kill sick people groaning under walls; / Sometimes I go about and poison wells."*[8] Not subtle. The audience knows whom to root for, and it isn't the person poisoning wells at nighttime.

Shylock, however, has no such overbearing characteristics. We are told he is an overbearing parent, but we are also given reason to support this overprotectiveness in the fact that his daughter is spirited away by the Christians (employed by Antonio) so his overprotection seems warranted. We are told he values money over all else (playing on an old and awful ethnic stereotype) and yet time and again, Shylock shows a disregard for money in favor of more important, loftier ideals: loyalty, fairness, family.

In short, over and over, Shylock subverts prejudiced expectations. His character arc is designed to show the inhumanity of prejudice.

Take, for instance, when he hears that his daughter, Jessica, has not only stolen much of his fortune but also taken his dead wife's engagement ring. Shylock is told Jessica has sold it already, for a monkey—a concrete detail designed to juxtapose a symbol of fidelity and honor, traded for something utterly frivolous. Shylock, when he hears the news, has a very human, lost reaction:

TUBAL One of them showed me a ring that he had of your daughter for a monkey.
SHYLOCK Out upon her! Thou torturest me, Tubal. It was my turquoise. I had it
of Leah when I was a bachelor. I would not have given it for a wilderness of
monkeys.[9]

This reaction is unnecessary to the plot of the play, unless Shakespeare wanted to provide real motivation for Shylock's lust for revenge. It is Act I when we hear that Antonio has spit on him and called him a dog, and it is Act I wherein Antonio says he'll continue to do it because Shylock is a Jew. That should be enough. It's more than Richard III gets, definitely, in terms of villainous motivation.

But throughout the next acts, we are given ample motivation for Shakespeare's supposed antagonist. Antonio's employees plot to lure

Shylock out of the house so Jessica may flee and elope with the Christian, Lorenzo. These Christians, like Bassanio, don't want Jessica for the person she is, but for the ducats she brings. This further suggests the Christians in the play see marriage as a purely economic exchange. Neither Lorenzo nor Bassanio ever show remorse for marrying women for their money. Shylock's diction, however, suggests a loyalty to his dead wife, Leah. A loyalty his daughter cared for not a jot.

ANTONIO *But little. I am armed and well prepared.—*
  Give me your hand, Bassanio. Fare you well.
  Grieve not that I am fall'n to this for you,
  For herein Fortune shows herself more kind
  Than is her custom. It is still her use
  To let the wretched man outlive his wealth,
  To view with hollow eye and wrinkled brow
  An age of poverty— from which lingering penance
  Of such misery doth she cut me off.
  Commend me to your honorable wife.
  Tell her the process of Antonio's end.
  Say how I loved you. Speak me fair in death.
  And when the tale is told, bid her be judge
  Whether Bassanio had not once a love.
  Repent but you that you shall lose your friend,
  And he repents not that he pays your debt.
  For if the Jew do cut but deep enough,
  I'll pay it presently with all my heart.
BASSANIO *Antonio, I am married to a wife*
  \Which is as dear to me as life itself.
  But life itself, my wife, and all the world
  Are not with me esteemed above thy life.
  I would lose all—ay, sacrifice them all
  Here to this devil—to deliver you.
PORTIA *Your wife would give you little thanks for that*
  If she were by to hear you make the offer.
GRATIANO *I have a wife, whom I protest I love.*
  I would she were in heaven, so she could
  Entreat some power to change this currish Jew.
  NERISSA *'Tis well you offer it behind her back.*
  The wish would make else an unquiet house.
SHYLOCK *[aside] These be the Christian husbands. I have a daughter.*
  Would any of the stock of Barabbas
  Had been her husband rather than a Christian!—
  We trifle time. I pray thee, pursue sentence.[10]

While our "heroes" reveal the superficiality of their understanding of marriage—something fluid and transactional, a bond that can be traded and moved for their liking, Shylock stands aghast at their lack of maturity. Beyond this, his immediate response is anchored in abhorrence that these are the type of flighty, dismissive men that his daughter is now married to.

Shakespeare doesn't have to include these moments for Shylock. They only serve to create true empathy and pathos for Shylock, even when he is about to do something abhorrent himself. The inclusion of the entire Jessica subplot serves to humanize and motivate Shylock in a way the audience can understand. Why do that, if not to draw attention to the human cost of Othering?

Consider, as an addition to their letter to Shylock, having students research how Shylock was portrayed on stage in the centuries leading up to World War II.

The productions' choices of "clown" don't match the language on the page. Why would, for hundreds of years, society not notice that what Shylock was saying was so much more important than what the audience thought they were seeing? What does the history of this character teach us about our biases blinding us to each other's humanity?

Activity Five: Annotating for the Cost of Otherness

If you prick us, do we not bleed?[11]

Finally, take Shylock's most well-known speech. Have students annotate it, looking for compelling evidence and characterization and motivation. Shylock does not have speeches like Barabas does, about doing evil in the darkness of night. No. When he demands honesty and transparency about what has happened to his daughter, even though Salanio and Salerio *know* Antonio's ships are wrecked, and his bond forfeit, they continue to bait Shylock, because they see his pain as inconsequential.

These two interchangeable and forgettable characters seem to exist in the play exclusively to humanize Shylock. Their inhuman insistence on seeing Shylock as "Other" seems to know no bounds. His human plight cannot be as serious as their own, because they do not think Shylock is as human as they are. Shylock's response is ready—in the face of Christian hypocrisy, he says this:

SALANIO Let me say "amen" betimes, lest the devil cross my prayer, for here he comes in the likeness of a Jew.

[enter SHYLOCK] How now, Shylock! what news among the merchants?
SHYLOCK You know, none so well, none so well as you, of my daughter's flight.
SALARINO That's certain: I, for my part, knew the tailor that made the wings she flew withal.

SALANIO And Shylock, for his own part, knew the bird was fledged; and then it is the complexion of them all to leave the dam.

SHYLOCK She is damned for it.

SALANIO That's certain, if the devil may be her judge.

SHYLOCK My own flesh and blood to rebel!

SALANIO Out upon it, old carrion! rebels it at these years?

SHYLOCK I say, my daughter is my flesh and blood.

SALARINO There is more difference between thy flesh and hers than between jet and ivory; more between your bloods than there is between red wine and rhenish. But tell us, do you hear whether Antonio have had any loss at sea or no?

SHYLOCK There I have another bad match: a bankrupt, a prodigal, who dare scarce show his head on the Rialto; a beggar, that was used to come so smug upon the mart; let him look to his bond: he was wont to call me usurer; let him look to his bond: he was wont to lend money for a Christian courtesy; let him look to his bond.

SALARINO Why, I am sure, if he forfeit, thou wilt not take his flesh: what's that good for?

SHYLOCK To bait fish withal: if it will feed nothing else, it will feed my revenge. He hath disgraced me, and hindered me half a million; laughed at my losses, mocked at my gains, scorned my nation, thwarted my bargains, cooled my friends, heated mine enemies; and what's his reason? I am a Jew. Hath not a Jew eyes? hath not a Jew hands, organs, dimensions, senses, affections, passions? fed with the same food, hurt with the same weapons, subject to the same diseases, healed by the same means, warmed and cooled by the same winter and summer, as a Christian is? If you prick us, do we not bleed? if you tickle us, do we not laugh? if you poison us, do we not die? and if you wrong us, shall we not revenge? If we are like you in the rest, we will resemble you in that. If a Jew wrong a Christian, what is his humility? Revenge. If a Christian wrong a Jew, what should his sufferance be by Christian example? Why, revenge. The villany you teach me, I will execute, and it shall go hard but I will better the instruction.[12]

There is certainly a lot to unpack there, and consider spending an entire day on this scene—the pacing, the panic, the disregard Salanio and Salerio show. But most importantly is the shining moment of rhetoric Shylock gives us. Note that the speech isn't at all complicated. Its diction is easy to understand; in fact, most of it is monosyllabic. Syntactically, it is fascinating because it is so obviously designed to be easily understood. The logic cannot be denied. If this be our antagonist (and it must be—this is the only guy trying to kill another guy in this play) what on earth is Shakespeare doing, making that murderous impulse so darn understandable?

THIS PLAY IS EITHER VERY FEMINIST
OR VERY ANTI-FEMINIST

Activity Six: A Close Reading of Gender Dynamics

I will have nothing else but only this;
And now methinks I have a mind to it.[13]

A word for and against Portia:

Portia is problematic. She is still revered as the ultimate Shakespearean heroine, in the midst of the Rosalinds and Violas and Beatrices. And this categorization makes sense, as she is in a comedy, and, as such, she is a woman who disguises herself to gain access to the male world, and once there, demonstrates her absolute ability to participate usefully within that domain from which she should, historically, be excluded.

Within this activity and these discussions, we want students to wrestle with Portia's heroic qualities in comparison with her more troublesome qualities. At the end of this examination, are students willing to view her as the heroine of the play? Why or why not? What they choose doesn't really matter; what we are aiming for is an appreciation of how she has traditionally been seen, and what a close reading of her character may reveal.

She's an interesting character, because unlike anyone else in Shakespeare's canon, she is inarguably freed by her marriage. Most comedies end with a wedding, and a bidding of goodnight to the audience so that the lovers may off to bed—*Merchant* marries the lovers midplay, separates them before the marriage is consummated, and returns them with the power dynamic within that marriage turned topsy-turvy.

Portia changes the most within the play, making her the best contender for protagonist of this particular text. When we meet her, she is utterly lacking in power or autonomy, and by marrying Bassanio, a weak man who can get nothing done on his own merit, she is free to rule the roost. This in itself is not problematic, and could be another example of Shakespeare using *The Merchant of Venice* to seriously subvert his audience's expectations of womanhood in an exciting way—indeed, that is the way criticism has treated Portia for years now. However, that generous reading ignores something else about Portia: a lust for power.

This is a play in which Portia (and, to lesser degrees Nerissa and Jessica) yearn for independence from their fathers—a feminist ideal, indeed! And yet, when independence is gained, they abuse their newfound independence, and behave cruelly and tyrannically; the opposite of what we would expect from the speaker of "The quality of mercy is not strain'd."[14]

Family dynamics are nothing new to Shakespeare, and within those family dynamics is the idea of rituals within families; there is no familial ritual
more explored than marriage. One reading of this ritual is that a daughter
goes from her father's house to her husband's house, and the ritual is passed
on in perpetuity for the betterment of society. Shakespeare has his heroines
subvert this expectation plenty of times, and it often turns tragic. Think of
Juliet taking marriage into her own hands, and excluding her parents—though
we understand *why* she does it, she still ends up dead.

This disrupting ritual is precisely what Shakespeare explores with two
mirror-image daughters: Portia and Jessica. In this play Shakespeare avoids
comedy and instead shows the audience what happens if the power structure
is not restored to the patriarchal norm by the time the curtain comes down.
Shakespeare's conclusion seems to be that the transgression away from the
subservient female within the play creates chaos and disruption of the natural
order, resulting in tragedy for the men of the family unit.

Portia is often revered as a woman in Shakespeare's drama who is
designed to demonstrate the cleverness of women, particularly the superiority of women's wits when pitted against the man's world in which they live.
Within the play itself, she is universally lauded with such language as "she
is fair, and, fairer than that word, of wondrous virtues." Such diction attributed to Portia is perhaps ironic and misleading, since Portia, though "fair"
in beauty, is never authentically fair in life. She always ensures she comes
out on top.

By marrying a man as weak as Bassanio, she can become both master and
mistress of Belmont and is finally free from her dead father's mandates. Her
marriage midplay untethers her to gendered expectations of behavior and
identity. She can embody both male and female roles, and does, immediately,
in the courtroom scene.

Indeed, when Act V takes us back to the magic and moonlight of Belmont,
Portia is staunchly in control. Her first line in Act V is "The light we see is
burning in my hall,"[15] with no mention of how everything that was once hers
now belongs to Bassanio. She is clearly running the show by subverting the
marriage ritual to her liking. When it is revealed that her wedding ring was
given to honor Antonio rather than honor their marriage, she shames them
both by asking Antonio to "Give him this and bid him keep it better than the
other."[16]

Her insistence that Antonio act as the "surety" seems to indicate a demand
on Portia's part on the relinquishment of the homosocial and perhaps homoerotic bond between Bassanio and Antonio. Including Antonio in the belittling and humiliating role of handing Bassanio Portia's wedding ring and
insisting he tell him, in front of her, he needs to keep it better this time leaves
no question as to who is dominant in the marriage.

Portia has subverted the dominance of the patriarchal society. The last act centers on her alone ensuring that the ring motif of the play is concluded. Rings don't mean fidelity and loyalty and devotion (as they do for Shylock) they mean power and sex and bawdy humor. And the men of the play, Antonio and Bassanio, have nothing to do in Act V except following Portia's orders.

Don't misunderstand—an empowered woman who is empowered within her marriage is not a bad thing. It is certainly a radical, subversive choice for Shakespeare to make, but that in itself is not problematic.

It is that Portia preaches what we, as people, should be within her speech, "The Quality of Mercy is Not Strain'd." That's the heroic moment in the text—a woman infiltrates a man's space, and wins by using a supposedly feminine ideal of mercy. She says we should do what is right for others, not because it helps us, but because doing for others what is right is the best thing a person can do for another person. It's a beautiful, lyrical speech. And critics to this day seem to think because Portia says it, Portia must mean it—a type of subtle misogyny that remains troublesome.

At this point, have students create a T-chart for Portia. On one side, they should track what she says. On the other side, have them track what she does. From the moment of her marriage onward to the curtain coming down, what does she say, and what does she do? And what are we to infer about her character from that disconnect?

Portia doesn't, for instance, ever act on her own advice. Have students re-read or, better yet, perform Act IV and count every time Portia says, "Tarry, Jew/The law has yet another hold on you."[17] Portia doesn't care about *why* Shylock would go to these extremes. She doesn't care about what Antonio has done to enable this hatred. She doesn't even seem to mind that Antonio is scared, and Bassanio is distraught. Her pacing and repetition and syntax in that scene convey her basking in power—a power that, once found, she is not giving up.

So what then, was Shakespeare trying to show us? In a play full of disguises and misunderstood intentions and power plays, in a play that defies description because it simultaneously caters to genres while subverting them at the same time, what are we to understand about Portia?

Consider that every character who knew themselves at the beginning has lost themselves at the end (Shylock, for example). And characters who seemed lost and without a clear identity in the beginning have certainly solidified their understanding of self, but at the sacrifice of doing wrong to another. Portia, our problematic heroine, is resolved as the head of the household, the hero of the courtroom, and the ruler in her marriage.

She has found herself, and what she has found is someone who enjoys lording power over others. Bassanio has found himself as not the lord of Belmont, but the rescued weakling who knows (and is meant to know) he owes all he enjoys in life to Portia. And Antonio, who claims in Act One to not know why he is so sad, knows Bassanio knows he loves him and would die for him, and, in the end, knows he has to let Bassanio go—Portia will tolerate nothing less. Their identities have solidified, but their characters are not necessarily the better for it.

Perhaps the answer is one again in that seemingly distracting casket test: it personifies disguise in the play. People in this text are not what they appear to be, just as those caskets are not what they appear to be. Jessica is no dutiful daughter, Shylock is no murderous Barabas, Antonio is no victim, Bassanio is no ardent lover, and Portia is no real hero, even if the word "fair" gets plastered to her over and over again. We are all in disguise, and our disguises are useful in getting what we want. Just ask all the characters within *The Merchant of Venice*.

WRITTEN IN 1596, 1857, 1943, AND TODAY

Activity Seven: This Is How It Happens.
Tracing Syntax in Tyranny

Which is the merchant here, and which the Jew?[18]

Every genocide in modern history has begun first with the Othering of a group of people. This Othering occurs first at a syntactical level. The power structure that seeks to expel and separate starts using words or phrases that dehumanize the Othered. In *The Merchant of Venice*, Portia says "Shylock" only once. The rest of the time she says, "The Jew." That is, until she ups the ante and calls him an "alien."[19] This diction is purposeful. It's easier to destroy someone if you don't think they are the same type of person as you and yours.

When asked to see current parallels to syntactical Othering, students often mention gang problems within their own student community. Syntactical Otherness and tribalism are used to recruit others to gain loyalty and safety, but the cost is the clear implication that other groups are therefore fair game to "hunt." Students are seeing a modern-day example of the very human cost of these fictitious differences between peers in their hallways right now. It is a powerful recognition for them to see the simultaneous draw of such an institution, and the cost of perpetuating a system that has power only by excluding and dehumanizing others.

This system of syntactical oppression, though still visible, certainly isn't new. And it isn't only in the arts. Syntactical oppression has a rich history of showing up in primary documents that form the basis for legal discrimination—or worse.

As a group, analyze the language in the Dred Scott Decision: Annotate the decision for syntactical Othering, and then facilitate a conversation about how language is being used to justify tribalism and dehumanizing Otherness.

Majority Opinion (7-2), Dred Scott v. Sanford, 1857

   The language of the Declaration of Independence is . . . conclusive: . . . "We hold these truths to be self-evident: that all men are created equal." . . .[I]t is too clear for dispute, that the enslaved African race were not intended to be included, and formed no part of the people who framed and adopted this declaration. . . . They perfectly understood the meaning of the language they used, and how it would be understood by others; and they knew that it would not in any part of the civilized world be supposed to embrace the negro race, which, by common consent, had been excluded from civilized Governments and the family of nations, and doomed to slavery. . . . The brief preamble [to the Constitution] . . . declares that it is formed by the people of the United States; that is to say, by those who were members of the different political communities in the several States; and its great object is declared to be to secure the blessings of liberty to themselves and their posterity. It speaks in general terms of the people of the United States, and of citizens of the several States, when it is providing for the exercise of the powers granted or the privileges secured to the citizen. It does not define what description of persons are intended to be included under these terms, or who shall be regarded as a citizen and one of the people. . . . [T]here are two clauses in the Constitution which point directly and specifically to the negro race as a separate class of persons, and show clearly that they were not regarded as a portion of the people or citizens of the Government then formed. [T]he right of property in a slave is distinctly and expressly affirmed in the Constitution. The right to traffic in it, like an ordinary article of merchandise and property, was guaranteed to the citizens of the United States, in every State that might desire it, for twenty years. And the Government in express terms is pledged to protect it in all future time, if the slave escapes from his owner. This is done in plain words—too plain to be misunderstood. And no word can be found in the Constitution which gives Congress a greater power over slave property, or which entitles property of that kind to less protection than property of any other description. The only power conferred is the power coupled with the duty of guarding and protecting the owner in his rights.[20]

Assign students a class period (or more—you know your students) to research primary source material, annotate it, and come up with evidence of syntactical Othering. You can make a list of historical documents, but we suggest interspersing it with current events as well, to demonstrate how close reading of modern-day injustice is vital.

Some Possible Examples

Adolf Hitler, quoted in "Hitler," by Joachim Fest, Vintage Books Edition, 1974, p. 679-680:

Nature is cruel; therefore we are also entitled to be cruel. When I send the flower of German youth into the steel hail of the next war without feeling the slightest regret over the precious German blood that is being spilled, should I not also have the right to eliminate millions of an inferior race that multiplies like vermin?[21]

*Speeches by Reichsfuehrer-SS **Himmler** before senior SS officers in Poznan, October 4 and 6, 1943.*

I mean the evacuation of the Jews, the extermination of the Jewish race. It's one of those things it is easy to talk about, "the Jewish race is being exterminated," says one party member, "that's quite clear, it's in our program, elimination of the Jews, and we're doing it, exterminating them." And then they come, 80 million worthy Germans, and each one has his decent Jew. Of course the others are vermin, but this one is an A-1 Jew. Not one of those who talk this way has watched it, not one of them has gone through it. Most of you know what it means when 100 corpses are lying side by side, or 500, or 1,000. To have stuck it out and at the same time—apart from exceptions caused by human weakness—to have remained decent fellows, that is what has made us hard. This is a page of glory in our history which has never been written and is never to be written.

I ask of you that what I say in this circle you really only hear and never speak of. We come to the question: how is it with the women and the children? I have resolved even here on a completely clear solution. That is to say I do not consider myself justified in eradicating the men—so to speak killing or ordering them killed—and allowing the avengers in the shape of the children to grow up for our sons and grandsons. The difficult decision has to be taken, to cause this Volk [people] to disappear from the earth.[22]

The above examples demonstrate how syntactically exact and purposeful oppressive forces must be in the identifying and Othering of people before they can be legally, socially, mortally removed.

Figure 1.1 provides a sample annotation of the Hitler quotation above. The sample demonstrates the identification of multiple authorial choices in a short, two-sentence passage. This process of annotation will prepare a student to discuss the significance of the text, either verbally or in writing.

After research has been done, have students write a simple paragraph comparing Act IV (or any part they choose, if they have something else in mind) of *The Merchant of Venice* to their historical text. What similarities can be found?

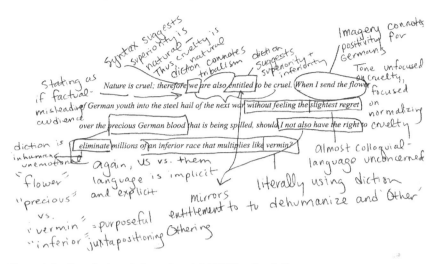

Figure 1.1   Sample Annotation of an Adolf Hitler Quotation.

And what do these syntactic similarities suggest? And, most importantly, why does Shakespeare do this? What is he trying to accomplish for his audiences?

CONCLUSION

Ultimately, *The Merchant of Venice* serves as a very savvy subversive missive about the dangers and realities of Otherness and tribalism. Any time we lean into being included, we are implicitly excluding. And anytime anyone is excluded, there is an "us" and "them" dynamic set in motion. Shylock is wrong to seek bloody revenge, but he's not wrong to be so mad. He was wronged, broken, dismayed by these Christians in the play. They robbed him, stole his daughter, and then asked for mercy. It's a troubling play, because it is so hard to root against Shylock, which we must do, because an eye for an eye leaves us all blind.

Perhaps Shakespeare's major lesson here is that society creates its own nightmares when it tries to insulate from them. The need to know who we are and what that means cannot be at the expense of others—for whatever safety it grants us will be fleeting, and those we have excluded, as we ourselves have been excluded know, it is a pain that is hard to forget.

NOTES

1. William Shakespeare, *The Merchant of Venice*, ed. Alan Durband (Hauppauge, NY: Barron's, 1985), 156.

2. Shakespeare, *The Merchant of Venice*, 108.

3. Heather C. McGhee, "Racism Has a Cost for Everyone," TED, accessed July 16, 2020, https://www.ted.com/talks/heather_c_mcghee_racism_has_a_cost_for_everyone.

4. Shakespeare, *The Merchant of Venice*, 156.

5. Shakespeare, *The Merchant of Venice*, 178.

6. Shakespeare, *The Merchant of Venice*, 92. My emphasis here and in other quotations that follow each activity throughout the book.

7. Shakespeare, *The Merchant of Venice*, 110.

8. Christopher Marlowe, *The Jew of Malta* (S.l.: WW NORTON, 2020).

9. Shakespeare, *The Merchant of Venice*, 112.

10. Shakespeare, *The Merchant of Venice*, 170–2.

11. Shakespeare, *The Merchant of Venice*, 110.

12. Shakespeare, *The Merchant of Venice*, 106–10.

13. Shakespeare, *The Merchant of Venice*, 182.

14. Shakespeare, *The Merchant of Venice*, 164.

15. Shakespeare, *The Merchant of Venice*, 194.

16. Shakespeare, *The Merchant of Venice*, 206.

17. Shakespeare, *The Merchant of Venice*, 176.

18. Shakespeare, *The Merchant of Venice*, 164.

19. Shakespeare, *The Merchant of Venice*, 176.

20. Roger B Taney, "The Dred Scott Decision: Opinion of Chief Justice Taney," The Library of Congress, accessed July 16, 2020, https://www.loc.gov/item/17001543/.

21. Joachim Fest, *Hitler* (New York, NY: Houghton Mifflin, 2013), 679–80.

22. Peter Padfield, *Himmler: Reichsführer-SS* (London: Thistle Publishing, 2013), 469.

Chapter 2

Systemic Racial Injustice and *A Raisin in the Sun*

This chapter will model how pairing a literary text with nonfiction texts not only allows the teacher to cover literary and informational reading standards in the same unit but also leads students to a deeper, more useful understanding of the literature being studied and the issues being discussed. Specifically, the unit described in this chapter will pair Lorraine Hansberry's 1959 play *A Raisin in the Sun* with Ta-Nehisi Coates's 2014 *Atlantic Monthly* article "The Case for Reparations"[1]—as well as other nonfiction sources—for the purpose of exploring systemic racial injustice and Otherness.

This layering of nonfiction onto our literary work will demonstrate that a unit centered on a play, novel, or poet can also help students meet the standards for informational reading (literature and nonfiction do not *have to be* taught separately).

Applying the ideas in this chapter does not *require* that you teach this particular play paired with this particular nonfiction article. Rather, the chapter will

- model how a universal concept—such as *Otherness*—along with its causes and consequences, can be explored through the study of a literary text.
- model how the study of relevant informational texts can be layered onto the study of a literary text.

As discussed in the Introduction, this chapter will not end our discussion of Otherness, as many of the issues in our "sea of troubles" have Otherness at their root. This chapter, like the previous chapter and those that follow, will also explore the relationship between Otherness and language—to what extent is Otherness supported by language? Created by language?

Teaching literary versus informational texts is often presented to teachers (and to students) as a choice, as if one does not reflect the other. But keeping them in separate boxes will result in a more superficial understanding of either text and, beyond this, a missed opportunity to explore the connections between them—both in content and skill development.

OTHERNESS AND SOCIOECONOMIC INJUSTICE IN U.S. HOUSING POLICIES

A discussion of Otherness (and the inequality that results from it) in Lorraine Hansberry's *A Raisin in the Sun* will center on two policies from the first half of the twentieth century:

• Redlining
• Restrictive Covenants

Many students may not be familiar with these terms, but there are a variety of sources available to help students understand them. For example, "The Case for Reparations" discusses these policies and their effects at length, creating an opportunity to combine the study of literature with the study of a work of nonfiction (in this case, a work by one of the most important contemporary writers in America). Students can access Coates's article online from *The Atlantic*, and the essay is also collected in Coates's 2017 book, *We Were Eight Years in Power*.

In addition, the website *Mapping Inequality*[2] provides an interactive map of redlining in American cities.

For students in California, Josh Begley's site *Redlining California*[3] allows students to explore a "redlined" version of Google Maps as well as the original redlining maps and documents.

At the time this chapter was being written, the Democratic primaries for the 2020 Presidential election were underway, and one of the candidates, Michael Bloomberg, received criticism for a comment that had surfaced from his past. In the comment, Bloomberg seemed to suggest that ending "redlining" had, in part, caused the 2008 financial crisis. In the comment, Bloomberg characterized redlining as the denial of mortgage loans to people in poverty or without credit.

Students should know that such a characterization is inaccurate. The policy of redlining was based on racism. Poverty and lack of credit for people of color are its effects, not its basis.

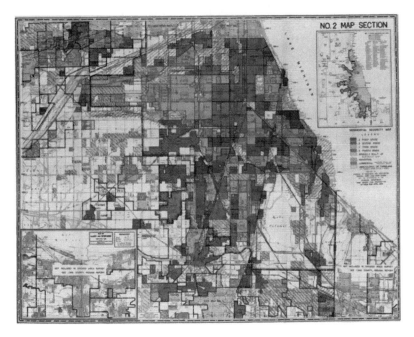

Figure 2.1   Redlining Map of Southside Chicago.

Figure 2.1 provides a redlined map of Southside Chicago, where *A Raisin in the Sun* is set. In the map, individual neighborhoods are "graded" as A, B, C, or D. Coates explains these grades, as well as their context, in his article:

> *In 1934, Congress created the Federal Housing Administration. The FHA insured private mortgages, causing a drop in interest rates and a decline in the size of the down payment required to buy a house. . . . The FHA [. . .] adopted a system of maps that rated neighborhoods according to their perceived stability. On the maps, green areas, rated "A," indicated "in demand" neighborhoods that, as one appraiser put it, lacked "a single foreigner or Negro." These neighborhoods were considered excellent prospects for insurance. Neighborhoods where black people lived were rated "D" and were usually considered ineligible for FHA backing. They were colored in red. Neither the percentage of black people living there nor their social class mattered. Black people were viewed as a contagion.*

By studying the primary documents that accompany redlining maps (such as in the activities below), students will discover that the diction and syntax used in these documents fully support Coates's claim that the Federal Housing Administration viewed African Americans and other minorities as "a contagion."

Activity One: Redlining in Your (and Your Students') Own City

Been thinking that we maybe could meet the notes on a little old two-story somewhere, with a yard where Travis could play in the summertime, if we use part of the insurance for a down payment and everybody kind of pitch in.[4]

Most American cities were "redlined" in the 1930s or 1940s, and in most cases the makeup of those cities today still reflects those lines. If you are not teaching in Chicago, where *A Raisin in the Sun* is set and which Coates discusses at length, then a good place to begin is exploring redlining and its effects in the city where your students live.

For example, the authors of this book teach in a city in Northern California. When our students view redlining maps of the city made in the late 1930s, they find that our school sits in an area graded D, and, for most of our students, the neighborhoods in which they live are graded either C or D.

Similar maps exist for most American cities. The *Mapping Inequality* interactive map allows students to hover over their own neighborhoods and read the language used to justify these grades. Through the *Redlining California* website, students are able to access images of the original documents that accompanied the maps.

For example, when our students hover over the section of the map where our school is located, they find that the FHA used the following language to justify a grade of D:

- "Detrimental Influences: Heterogeneous improvements and population."
- "Infiltration of subversive races exists."
- "This area largely given over to lower racial elements."

Students should discuss the specific diction used in these primary documents, and the effect of that diction. Specifically, students should analyze the extent to which *language* in these documents creates *Otherness* that becomes the basis for *inequality*. When discussing this language, students should recognize the *dehumanizing* effects of the language. For example, diction such as *detrimental, heterogeneous, infiltration,* and *subversive* are loaded with connotation and subtext and therefore warrant discussion.

Studying these redlining maps and the primary documents that accompany them will also introduce students to the concept of "deed restrictions"—a phrase found repeatedly in FHA documents—also known as "restrictive covenants."

In "The Case for Reparations," Coates explains not only that the presence of African Americans in a neighborhood resulted in a grade of D but also that in order to receive a grade higher than D, a neighborhood had to have a restrictive covenant—an agreement that no properties would be sold to people of color.

This is demonstrated when our students hover over a "green" area of the map that was graded A. That section is described as a "highly deed restricted area."

Coates goes on to explain that, because of the policies of redlining and restrictive covenants, African Americans were essentially locked out of the home mortgage market, locked out of neighborhoods that benefited from more and more investment, and locked into *ghettos*.

Coates states: "The implications are chilling. As a rule, poor black people do not work their way out of the ghetto—and those who do often face the horror of watching their children and grandchildren tumble back."

Activity Two: Socratic Seminar

It's just a plain little old house—but it's made good and solid—and it will be ours. Walter Lee—it makes a difference in a man when he can walk on floors that belong to him.[5]

An effective method for exploring these issues with students is a Socratic Seminar, which is exactly what it sounds like: a meeting in which the participants employ the Socratic method of seeking truth through questions.

There are many resources out there for conducting a Socratic Seminar. Both the National Council of Teachers of English (NCTE) and Advancement Via Individual Determination (AVID) have developed strategy guides for this method.[6] But the structure of a Socratic Seminar is fairly simple: give the students a meaty topic, put them in a circle, and start asking questions.

Simple, but not easy. Many students would rather write a ten-page essay than speak in front of their classmates, but this strategy can be very effective and very powerful if given time to breathe.

When students engage in a Socratic Seminar, they should know that they are not engaging in a debate, but rather collaborating in an inquiry. They should also know that their purpose is not to answer or solve a complex question or problem; rather, their purpose is to open up and explore and analyze.

It is helpful if students have a specific text or research notes to reference during a Socratic Seminar. In the case of the Socratic Seminar described below, students were asked to conduct research in order to answer the following essential questions:

• What are the long-term effects of housing policy on poverty in the United States?
• Why is a higher percentage of the Black population in the United States below the poverty level?
• Why are Black citizens incarcerated at a higher percentage than other groups in the United States?

To guide their research, students were given links to the following articles (for use in addition to Coates's "The Case for Reparations") but were also encouraged to allow their research to take them in other directions, always with our essential questions in mind.

- "The Racist Housing Policy That Made Your Neighborhood" by Alexis C. Madrigal, *The Atlantic Monthly*, May 22, 2014.[7]
- "How We Built the Ghettos: A Brief Introduction to America's Long History of Racist Housing Policy" by Jamelle Bouie, *The Daily Beast*, July 12, 2017.[8]
- "Supreme Court vs. Neighborhood Segregation" by Alana Semuels, *The Atlantic Monthly*, June 5, 2015.[9]
- "The Widening Racial Wealth Divide" by James Surowiecki, *The New Yorker*, October 3, 2016.[10]
- "Historian Says Don't 'Sanitize' How Our Government Created Ghettos," *NPR's Fresh Air*, May 14, 2015.[11]
- "From Ferguson to Baltimore: The Fruits of Government-Sponsored Segregation" by Richard Rothstein, *Economic Policy Institute*, April 29, 2015.[12]

Also, as previously described, students were led to information about housing policy and racial disparity in their own community, using the aforementioned *Mapping Inequality* and *Redlining California* websites as well as the *Statistical Atlas* website (https://statisticalatlas.com).[13]

Sample Socratic Seminar Transcript

The following is a small portion of a transcript from a Socratic Seminar conducted with twelfth grade students in 2017.

Student 1: *Okay, so the first thing I want to talk about is redlining. Redlining is, as you guys know, like a cutout of each city that defines the zones that are either a red zone, which is not worth spending any tax money or giving any loans to. Those are the areas that are usually really rundown, really poor. Those areas are also defined as having minorities in them. Then there is the yellow zone which is on the decline. Yellow zones had some minorities, but not always. They were zones that only, as was described in Mapping Inequalities by Richmond University, yellow zones were places that only—in quotations—"dumb" loan businesses or taxpayers would invest in, and then blue and green zones were generally seen as places that most companies would loan out money to, usually white families or houses in these nicer areas.*

Student 2: *I'd also like to add on that redlining is, as you said, to see what areas have better levels of security, and it's based off of real estate businesses giving mortgages in the neighborhoods, and we see that it's usually segregated based off of race and income and ethnicity. So, as [Student 1] mentioned, the green and the blue were more desirable areas than the yellow and red. We also see that the Federal Housing Administration has a great influence on this. It was run from 1934 to 1968, and it is kind of solidifying racial segregation, and it's for helping people buy houses who meet certain requirements, so whoever meets the requirements are more likely to get the loans and the mortgages that they need in order to buy houses. And we see that African Americans usually didn't meet the requirements at the time, so they weren't receiving all of the loans that they needed in order to buy the houses.*

Student 3: *Adding on to the Federal Housing Administration, the reason why it promoted segregation, or at least made it worse, is because it only guaranteed loans to white people, and the Federal Housing Administration justified it by saying that if Blacks bought homes in suburban areas, property values of homes that were supposed to be for whites would decline in value, but it wasn't based off of any studies, so it was just based on discrimination and racism.*

Student 2: *So also, in the article "Supreme Court versus Neighborhood Segregation," in* The Atlantic, *which was published in 2015, they talk about the Inclusive Communities Project. So basically the state of Texas chose where to put projects—for example, they chose to give many projects in low-income areas, which led to the belief that more money was going to lower-income areas, causing more segregation, and the goal of the Inclusive Community Project was to revitalize a community and promote integration, and we also see—I did independent research as well—and we see that the Inclusive Community Project came up with the conclusion that they were against Texas just having to give money to projects that were going to continue in impoverished areas while the other areas did not have the same kind of projects.*

Student 4: *We can see that racial covenants were another tool that forced black people to stick to one neighborhood. Basically, racial covenants forbid property sales to African Americans and other minorities. This also was the Federal Housing Administration, which "financed mass production of building of subdivisions," which had started already in the 1930s, 1940s, and 1950s.*

Student 1: *To add to this, the Supreme Court ruling that we saw, to some extent it is the same as it was back in the 1930s, 1940s, and 1950s. According to* Daily Beast, *the article "How We Built the Ghettos," published in 2014, redlining was not only a way to divide up low-income areas from high-income areas, but it was also a way to figure out where to put money into or put business projects into. As most buildings were being built in the lower-income areas, as it was cheaper and it was also less aesthetically pleasing. They wanted to keep the good neighborhoods looking better than the impoverished neighborhoods, but also this redlining project, as well as the Federal Housing Administration, that whole process was done in order to put minorities in the lower-income areas, like force them in that direction. As loans and houses were being built in good neighborhoods, they could not be sold to low-income people or sold to minorities, whereas the businesses in the low-income areas, or the low-income houses were forced upon minorities. This is one reason the ghettos were built and it's one reason there's still problems with ghettos or the way that money is divided up among projects in any city, as we see today.*

Student 2: *So, in the same article we see that they talked about blockbusting and how it was kind of segregated between ethnicities because of the income levels that a family had, so we see that white neighborhoods were mainly higher income and that other ethnicities and minority races had lower incomes, and blockbusting was basically just having realtors letting minorities move in and have a chance to move into white neighborhoods, which were a little more expensive to move into, so we see that the white families would go to a different neighborhood, so the segregation just continued, and I just wanted to ask what everyone's opinion on that was, and how you think that these realtors would be able to do that?*

Student 5: *I was going to add to the blockbusting: these realtors would use strategies such as bringing minorities into the white neighborhoods and just walking them around because white people were afraid that since these minorities were from different areas, like the slums and the ghettos, that they would bring bad to their area, that would cause the movement of whites . . .*

Student 2: *White flight?*

Student 5: *. . .white flight from those areas, and these realtors would sell the houses that white people moved out of to minorities for initially a very low price, but they would mark up the prices over 100 to 200 percent.*

APPLYING KNOWLEDGE FROM
RESEARCH TO HANSBERRY'S PLAY

Now that students have conducted research, interacted with multiple informational texts, and engaged in a Socratic Seminar, they are ready to connect their learning to the literary text, in this case, Lorraine Hansberry's *A Raisin in the Sun*.

Activity Three: Considering the Play's Title

What happens to a dream deferred?
> *Does it dry up*
> *like a raisin in the sun?*
> *Or fester like a sore—*
> *And then run?*
> *Does it stink like rotten meat?*
> *Or crust and sugar over—*
> *like a syrupy sweet?*
>
> *Maybe it just sags*
> *like a heavy load.*

Or does it explode?

The title of Hansberry's play is taken from a line of Langston Hughes's poem, "Harlem," which is sometimes referred to as "A Dream Deferred." Therefore, it would be both appropriate and useful to take a look at the poem both before and after reading the play.

For example, you could ask students to make predictions about the play based upon their reading of the poem. What does Hughes mean, in this poem, by a *dream*? What does each image in the poem suggest, or represent? What, specifically, does the image of the "raisin in the sun" represent?

As students read the play, they may also notice—and it is certainly worth discussing—that the play's protagonist, Walter Lee Younger, progresses through the stages laid out in the poem: he festers, he sugars over, he sags, he explodes. And, of course, the play is premised on an insurance check that the family is expecting after Walter's father, before the play's start, has "dried up" and passed away.

After reading the play, return to the poem and ask students to discuss and/ or write about Hansberry's choice for the title of her play. What are the connections between the poem and the play?

Furthermore, ask students if they find connections between the poem and the research they have done about systematic racism and socioeconomic injustice in housing policy.

Figure 2.2 provides a redlined map of New York City, with the area of Harlem—all in red—indicated by the circle.

Whether or not Hughes was specifically thinking of housing policy when he wrote his 1951 poem, students can recognize that it is impossible not to consider the context of redlining when reading it, especially if homeownership is the most enduring emblem of the American Dream.

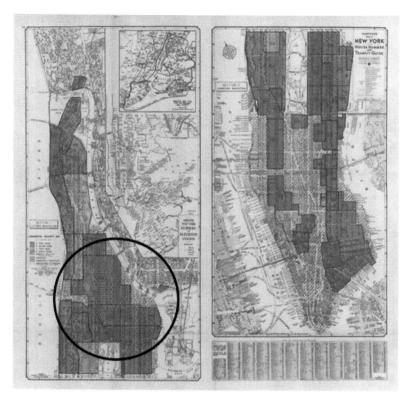

Figure 2.2   Redlining Map of New York City.

Segregation in Chicago

A Raisin in the Sun is set in Chicago, which Coates, in "The Case for Reparations," describes as one of the most segregated cities in the United States, a fact reinforced by CNN in a 2016 story titled, "Chicago: America's Most Segregated City."[14]

According to Coates, this segregation is not the result of a complex web of societal forces. Rather, it is specifically caused by restrictive covenants that banned African Americans in Chicago from receiving mortgage loans, and in the 1930s and 1940s, Chicago had more restrictive covenants—approximately half of all neighborhoods—than any other major American city.

Coates also explains that when restrictive covenants failed to keep people of color out, Chicago residents resorted to bombings and buyouts, both of which are reflected in Hansberry's play.

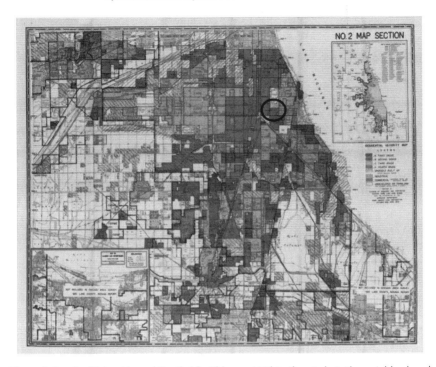

Figure 2.3   Redlining Map of Southside Chicago. Within the circle is the neighborhood of Washington Park (D78).

Activity Four: Researching *Hansberry v. Lee*

Well—it's what you might call a sort of welcoming committee, I guess. I mean they, we—I'm the chairman of the committee—go around and see the new people who move into the neighborhood and sort of give them the lowdown on the way we do things out in Clybourne Park.[15]

In the play, Lena Younger purchases a home for her family in the all-white neighborhood of Clybourne Park. Clybourne Park is fictional, but Hansberry based it on the Washington Park subdivision in Southside Chicago.

Figure 2.3 provides a redlined map of Southside Chicago. Within the circle is the neighborhood of Washington Park (D78), which the FHA describes as follows: "This is an area known as Washington Park sub-division in Woodlawn. This is a semi-blighted area and while it is restricted to whites, and the restriction having nine or ten years yet to run, there is a constantly increasing encroachment of Negroes from both the west and south."

In 1937, Lorraine Hansberry's father, Carl Hansberry, purchased a home in Washington Park, despite the restrictive covenant. Violent mobs formed. Lorraine Hansberry was eight years old at the time. In a 1964 letter to the *New York Times*, which students can also study as a primary document, she describes a rock coming through the window and nearly hitting her in the head, and her mother walking the halls at night armed with a pistol.

Carl Hansberry worked with NAACP lawyers to fight the restrictive covenant in a case—*Hansberry v. Lee*—that went all the way to the Supreme Court. There are several resources available for students to study this case, including the case brief itself[16] (which is available online but is challenging because of its legalese) and, perhaps more student-friendly, a 2013 post on the University of Chicago Library website titled, "Lorraine Hansberry: Her Chicago Law Story."[17]

- https://www.lib.uchicago.edu/about/news/lorraine-hansberry-her-chicago -law-story/

Block Associations: "The New Neighbors Orientation Committee"

It was Hansberry's personal experience, then, that inspired the story of the Younger family when they purchased a home in the all-white neighborhood of Clybourne Park.

Coates, in "The Case for Reparations," notes that when restrictive covenants were no longer effective in Chicago, residents of all-white neighborhoods began forming block associations that would compel other white homeowners not to sell their homes to African Americans and also compel African American families to sell their homes back.

Such was the case in *A Raisin in the Sun,* when Mr. Carl Lindner, representing the New Neighbors Orientation Committee of the Clybourne Park Improvement Association, visits the Youngers and argues that they would be happier with their own people.

Lindner offers, on behalf of the committee, to buy the house back at a higher price than Mama had just paid. Walter immediately throws Lindner out of the house, and it is this scene, in Act II, that sets up the play's climax and resolution in Act III.

In the following chapter, on intertextuality between *The Merchant of Venice* and *A Raisin in the Sun*, we will look more closely at the ways in which Otherness is supported by language in the scene with Mr. Lindner.

FINAL ESSAY

The following is an example of a culminating assignment for the study of *A Raisin in the Sun*, followed by a sample essay from a ninth grade student. This essay assignment requires students to draw meaningful connections between contemporary works of nonfiction and Hansberry's play.

Instructions: Write an essay in response to the following question: To what extent does the fictional story of the Younger family reflect the real-world experiences of African Americans, from the late 1950s, when *A Raisin in the Sun* was first produced, up to today?

Your response must include details from the play, *A Raisin in the Sun* (your primary source), and *at least four* of the following secondary sources:

- Source A: "This is What Racism Sounds Like in the Banking Industry." *The New York Times*. December 11, 2019.[18]
- Source B: "Chicago: America's Most Segregated City." CNN. January 5, 2016.
- Source C: "Discrimination in Housing against Nonwhites Persists Quietly, U.S. Study Finds." *The New York Times*. June 11, 2013.[19]
- Source D: "A Landmark Lesson in Being Black." *The New York Times*. March 7, 1999.[20]
- Source E: "The Case for Reparations." *The Atlantic Monthly*. June 2014."

Sample Student Essay

The following is a sample of a ninth grade student's response to the above prompt.

The True Fiction of Housing Discrimination

A Raisin in the Sun *is a 1959 play written by Lorraine Hansberry about the hardships of the fictional Younger family as they barely scrape by while dreaming of a better life. Their dreams relied heavily on Mama's check and how they were going to spend it. However, after the money goes missing, they are left with the only thing Mama purchased with it: a house in a white neighborhood. Although losing the money almost drives the family apart, the discrimination they faced for choosing to live there despite being different unites them in their pride of who they are. Fictional events the Youngers face from living in poverty to struggling to find a new home and to finally not being welcomed in a white neighborhood reflects the real housing discrimination African Americans from the late 1950s to today face.*

Living in poverty is something the Youngers and generations of African American families have in common. For instance, the Youngers are "plain people" employed as a driver and domestic workers (Hansberry 147). These jobs have the Youngers working for others, specifically white people, at a low wage. The importance of this is that although slavery is over, the Youngers are still serving an upper class, which instills the racist idea that they are less valuable. Also, the Youngers have been living in a roach-infested apartment in Southside Chicago with "cracking walls" and a "cramped little closet" for a kitchen for years (Hansberry 93). With the small amount they earn at work, the Youngers are not able to get anything better. This results in the Youngers remaining to live in poverty where it is hard to achieve much, and success is nothing but a dream.

Similarly, out of the African Americans living in Chicago, "more than a third . . . are poor" and "more than 30% are living in poverty" (Luhby). Being poor and living in poverty is an endless cycle the Youngers and other African Americans have a hard time breaking out of. A big chunk of African Americans living in poverty deepens the prejudice against them. It makes close-minded people feel like they are above them. Poverty being an endless cycle that causes discrimination is an experience both the Youngers and actual African Americans face.

The hard time Mama had looking for and purchasing housing represents a genuine struggle African Americans go through. For example, the best house Mama could find for "the least amount of money for [her] family" was in Clybourne Park, a neighborhood without any African Americans (Hansberry 93). This shows that non-African Americans are offered better housing and live in more agreeable conditions, unlike the more impoverished neighborhoods the Youngers are familiar with. The very distinct housing districts between African Americans and non-African Americans instill the prejudicial idea that African Americans deserve less than the rest, hence the restricted amount of houses presented to Mama.

Similarly, in a 1977 study of a "discrimination known as door-slamming . . . white testers were offered a unit when blacks were told that none were available" in 17 percent of the cases (Dewan). This shows that realtors favor white people, and do not take African Americans seriously. African Americans have a harder time purchasing houses that built their wealth, resulting in a majority remaining to live in poverty. Moreover, houses for African Americans "seem to cost twice as much as other houses" (Hansberry 93). The houses for African Americans are too expensive so that they will remain in poverty. Houses for non-African Americans are cheaper so that they can remain living in friendly neighborhoods. Although the house in the white neighborhood is the cheaper option, the discrimination and prejudice they will receive for merely being black and living there may not be worth it.

Likewise, compared to white borrowers, "black mortgage borrowers were charged higher interest rates" and "were denied mortgages that would have been approved for white applicants" (Flitter). The high prices of buying a house without a complicated mortgage discourage African Americans from even thinking of purchasing a house, which is a way to build wealth. This will contribute to the continuation of African Americans living in low-income housing districts and white people living among each other, which keeps the unending cycle of racism going. Not being able to purchase housing is a struggle African Americans have faced for years.

Not being accepted into a predominantly white neighborhood is an experience both the Youngers and real-life African American families have dealt with throughout the years. For instance, when Mr. Lindner, a "gentle" and "thoughtful" representative of the Clybourne Park Improvement Association, visited the Youngers, he offered to purchase their house. He suggested that "Negro families are happy in their own communities" (Hansberry 114, 118). Although Mr. Lindner is not blatantly racist, he wanted to pay the Youngers to leave his neighborhood, which shows that he is desperate to continue the racism instilled throughout the community for years. Segregation has become the norm in the Clybourne Park community; the thought of an African American family living there is a threat to their ignorant lifestyle. Moreover, African American families were being "bombed out of their" homes (Hansberry 100). This shows that people who have lived in segregation for years cannot stand the thought of living with someone of color. They would instead turn to violence than set aside their prejudice. Segregation feeds ignorance and creates racism, making integration nearly impossible.

Likewise, Lorraine Hansberry has experienced discrimination by merely living in a white neighborhood herself. She recalls being "spat at, cursed and pummeled in the daily trek to and from school" as well as watching "her mother [patrol] their house with a loaded pistol" against hateful mobs that "surrounded their home and once threw bricks at their windows" when she was only eight years old (Anderson). The Youngers' story seems so real because actual events the author faced in her childhood are the inspiration. This first-hand account allowed Hansberry to get down to the gritty details of being discriminated against for simply being African American in a world where integration is nearly impossible because of ignorance and hate. Being ostracized in a white community for being African American is an experience not isolated to the Youngers.

In conclusion, the housing discrimination the Youngers experienced in A Raisin in the Sun *illustrates the real-life struggles African Americans from the 1950s until now face. From living in an endless cycle of poverty, facing difficulties when looking for housing, and non-African American communities excluding them. Despite the 1950s being decades ago and the evolution of society, one thing remains the same: housing discrimination. Until this discrimination ends, the authentic experiences that transpired throughout* A Raisin in the Sun *will remain a true fiction.*

CONCLUSION

Hopefully, this chapter has illustrated not only the possibilities of layering the study of nonfiction texts into literary units but the vast opportunity such a simultaneous approach offers for learning.

Hansberry's tale of the Younger family fighting the machine of institutionalized, systematic oppression is powerful as it is. But when paired with students recognizing that they too are living, today, in neighborhoods structured by these same unjust systems, there comes a level of engagement and urgency that can be life changing. Though these systems of oppression are nearly a hundred years old, and though Hansberry's play is sixty years old, our students are still living in a world that is shaped by socioeconomic injustice created by those systems and illuminated by that play.

NOTES

1. Ta-Nehisi Coates, "The Case for Reparations," The Atlantic (Atlantic Media Company, June 2014), https://www.theatlantic.com/magazine/archive/2014/06/the-case-for-reparations/361631/.
2. "Mapping Inequality," Digital Scholarship Lab, accessed July 16, 2020, https://dsl.richmond.edu/panorama/redlining/.
3. Josh Begley, "Redlining California, 1936–1939," Redlining California, accessed July 16, 2020, https://joshbegley.com/redlining/.
4. Lorraine Hansberry, *A Raisin in the Sun* (New York, NY: Vintage Books, 2004), 44.
5. Hansberry, *A Raisin in the Sun*, 92.
6. "Socratic Seminars—ReadWriteThink," readwritethink.org, accessed July 16, 2020, http://www.readwritethink.org/professional-development/strategy-guides/socratic-seminars-30600.html.
7. Alexis C Madrigal, "The Racist Housing Policy That Made Your Neighborhood," The Atlantic (Atlantic Media Company, April 30, 2015), https://www.theatlantic.com/business/archive/2014/05/the-racist-housing-policy-that-made-your-neighborhood/371439/.
8. Jamelle Bouie, "How We Built the Ghettos," The Daily Beast (The Daily Beast Company, March 13, 2014), https://www.thedailybeast.com/how-we-built-the-ghettos.

9. Alana Semuels, "Supreme Court vs. Neighborhood Segregation," The Atlantic (Atlantic Media Company, July 13, 2015), https://www.theatlantic.com/business/arc hive/2015/06/supreme-court-inclusive-communities/396401/.

10. James Surowiecki, "The Widening Racial Wealth Divide," The New Yorker (The New Yorker, July 9, 2019), https://www.newyorker.com/magazine/2016/10/10/ the-widening-racial-wealth-divide.

11. "Historian Says Don't 'Sanitize' How Our Government Created Ghettos," NPR (NPR, May 14, 2015), https://www.npr.org/2015/05/14/406699264/historian -says-dont-sanitize-how-our-government-created-the-ghettos.

12. Richard Rothstein, "From Ferguson to Baltimore: The Fruits of Government-Sponsored Segregation," Economic Policy Institute, accessed April 29, 2015, https:/ /www.epi.org/blog/from-ferguson-to-baltimore-the-fruits-of-government-sponsored -segregation/.

13. "Overview of the United States," The Demographic Statistical Atlas of the United States—Statistical Atlas, accessed July 16, 2020, https://statisticalatlas.com/.

14. Tami Luhby, "Chicago: America's Most Segregated City," CNN Money (Cable News Network, January 5, 2016), https://money.cnn.com/2016/01/05/news/ec onomy/chicago-segregated/index.html.

15. Hansberry, *A Raisin in the Sun*, 115.

16. "Hansberry v. Lee," Casebriefs Hansberry v Lee Comments, accessed July 16, 2020, https://www.casebriefs.com/blog/law/civil-procedure/civil-procedure-keyed-to -marcus/establishing-the-structure-and-size-of-the-dispute/hansberry-v-lee-2/.

17. Lyonette Louis-Jacques, "Lorraine Hansberry: Her Chicago Law Story," The University of Chicago Library News—The University of Chicago Library, accessed March 6, 2013, https://www.lib.uchicago.edu/about/news/lorraine-hansberry-her-ch icago-law-story/.

18. Emily Flitter, "This Is What Racism Sounds Like in the Banking Industry," The New York Times (The New York Times, December 11, 2019), https://www.nyt imes.com/2019/12/11/business/jpmorgan-banking-racism.html.

19. Shaila Dewan, "Discrimination in Housing Against Nonwhites Persists Quietly, U.S. Study Finds," The New York Times (The New York Times, June 12, 2013), https://www.nytimes.com/2013/06/12/business/economy/discrimination-in-housing-against-nonwhites-persists-quietly-us-study-finds.html.

20. Michael Anderson, "A Landmark Lesson in Being Black," The New York Times (The New York Times, March 7, 1999), https://www.nytimes.com/1999/03 /07/theater/theater-a-landmark-lesson-in-being-black.html.

Chapter 3

Intertextuality in *The Merchant Of Venice* and *A Raisin in the Sun*

This chapter will model how to build a unit that uses intertextuality—specifically the pairing of two seemingly unlinked literary texts—to explore a universal concept. The chapter will pair William Shakespeare's *The Merchant of Venice* and Lorraine Hansberry's *A Raisin in the Sun*, two plays separated by centuries and continents, to explore socioeconomic injustice and Otherness.

Now, the previous two chapters have demonstrated how to tackle each of these texts individually—a perfectly reasonable choice. But now that we've walked through that possibility, consider which literary texts throughout the course of a year can be paired together to enhance student learning.

By focusing on the intertextuality between two seemingly separate works, students will see that concepts that have been learned in a particular unit are not, by any means, tethered only to that singular text. Othering defies space and time. It is, perhaps, a great equalizer among us.

Applying the ideas in this chapter does not *require* the pairing of these two plays, nor does it require that you teach *these* particular plays (or works in the particular genre of drama). Rather, the chapter will model

- how the universal concept of Otherness, along with its causes and consequences, can be explored through the study of a literary text,
- how the intertextual pairing of diverse literary texts can further enrich the exploration of a universal concept.

Studying universal concepts *intertextually* will provide students with

- a more authentic understanding of enduring literature and
- awareness that these issues are not tied to time and space (they are patterns that keep repeating).

- rigorous preparation for state testing:
  - Synthesizing
  - Choosing and citing evidence
  - Identifying main ideas
  - Comparing/contrasting
  - Interacting with multiple types of texts

ACTIVITY ONE: RESEARCHING THE ORIGIN OF THE *GHETTO*

I'll work twenty hours a day in all the kitchens in Chicago . . . I'll strap my baby to my back if I have to and scrub all the floors in America and wash all the sheets in America if I have to—but we got to MOVE! We got to get OUT OF HERE![1]

As discussed in the previous chapter, racist housing policies such as redlining, restrictive covenants, and blockbusting—beginning in the 1930s and 1940s—resulted in the segregation of American cities in ways that are still apparent today. In his essay "The Case for Reparations," Ta Nehisi Coates explains that, as mentioned in the previous chapter, African Americans were locked out of the home mortgage market and locked into ghettos.

This was a truth that Lorraine Hansberry, the author of *A Raisin in the Sun*, knew firsthand and that she reflected in her play.

In her book *To Be Young, Gifted and Black*, Lorraine Hansberry stated that "to be imprisoned in the ghetto is to be forgotten—or deliberately cheated of one's birthright—at best."[2]

An intertextual connection between Hansberry's *A Raisin in the Sun* and Shakespeare's *The Merchant of Venice* is the fact that the term *ghetto*, and ghettos themselves, originated in sixteenth-century Venice, the setting of *Merchant*. The Jewish citizens of Venice were only allowed to live in the small "foundry" (*geto* in Venetian) area of the city. Jews, like Shylock, were allowed to conduct business in the city during the day but were locked into the ghetto at night.

Indeed, Shylock's ability to conduct business is an important point to consider. One of the ways that Antonio has bated Shylock before the action of the play is by the constant loaning of money without interest, done purposefully to undercut Shylock's ability to make a living in one of the only professions allowed to the segregated Jewish population: moneylending. Shylock can't live where he wants, he can't conduct business as he wants, and he can't go where he wants. He has, on closer examination, quite a bit in common with the Younger family.

Whether you are teaching *Raisin* and *Merchant* in tandem or not, this presents an appropriate and useful research opportunity. Students can not only research the etymological history of the word but also compare conditions in urban ghettos in the United States with the original Jewish ghetto.

ACTIVITY TWO: COMPARING WALTER'S AND SHYLOCK'S SPEECHES

. . . I will better the instruction.[3]

Another intertextual connection between the two plays can be found by comparing a key speech by each play's central character.

In Act III of *A Raisin in the Sun*, we see a major reversal for the protagonist, Walter Lee Younger. After being swindled out of his father's pension, Walter decides to call Mr. Lindner, the representative of the Clybourne Park Welcoming Committee, back to the Younger apartment, with the intention of accepting his buyback offer.

When Walter's family protests, Walter gives a speech that runs parallel to a famous Shylock speech.

Figure 3.1 presents those two speeches side-by-side. Instruct students to read and compare the two speeches with the following focus question:

• What are the consequences of injustice?

One connection between the speeches is the idea of *instruction*. Walter Lee states that he has been *taught* by Willy Harris, who stole his money, to stop worrying over right and wrong. There are no right or wrong; there are only "takers" and the "tooken." In other words, Walter has been treated unjustly, and he will now, having learned his lesson, participate in that injustice.

Similarly, Shylock has a choice between mercy and revenge. He clearly knows that mercy is the right thing to do; however, he lists all the ways in which the Christians, including Antonio, have treated him unjustly. He also notes that if a Jew were to treat a Christian unjustly, the Christian would seek revenge. So why shouldn't he? Shylock, therefore, will "execute" the "villainy you teach me," demonstrating that Shylock, like Walter Lee, is passing on the injustice that he has received.

Students should recognize that in both cases, the character is driven to bad behavior that is taught to them by their oppressors, resulting in a cycle of injustice. And when we extend the examples of Shylock and Walter Lee to our larger society, we can conclude that the injustices inherent in our systems will only breed more injustice.

A Raisin in the Sun Act III	*The Merchant of Venice* Act III, Scene 1
WALTER	SHYLOCK
Talking 'bout life, Mama. You all always telling me to see life like it is. Well—I laid in there on my back today … and I figured it out. Life just like it is. Who gets and who don't get. (*He sits down with his coat on and laughs*) Mama, you know it's all divided up. Life is. Sure enough. Between the takers and the "tooken." (*He laughs*) I've figured it out finally. (*He looks around at them*) Yeah. Some of us always getting "tooken." (*He laughs*) People like Willy Harris, they don't never get "tooken." And you know why the rest of us do? 'Cause we all mixed up. Mixed up bad. We get to looking 'round for the right and the wrong; and we worry about it and cry about it and stay up nights trying to figure out 'bout the wrong and the right of things all the time … And all the time, man, them takers is out there operating, just taking and taking. Willy Harris? Shoot—Willy Harris don't even count. He don't even count in the big scheme of things. But I'll say one thing for old Willy Harris … he's taught me something. He's taught me to keep my eye on what counts in this world. Yeah—(*Shouting out a little*) Thanks, Willy! […] —there ain't nothing but taking in this world, and he who takes most is smartest—and it don't make a damn bit of difference how.	To bait fish withal: if it will feed nothing else, it will feed my revenge. He hath disgraced me, and hindered me half a million; laughed at my losses, mocked at my gains, scorned my nation, thwarted my bargains, cooled my friends, heated mine enemies; and what's his reason? I am a Jew. Hath not a Jew eyes? hath not a Jew hands, organs, dimensions, senses, affections, passions? fed with the same food, hurt with the same weapons, subject to the same diseases, healed by the same means, warmed and cooled by the same winter and summer, as a Christian is? If you prick us, do we not bleed? if you tickle us, do we not laugh? if you poison us, do we not die? and if you wrong us, shall we not revenge? If we are like you in the rest, we will resemble you in that. If a Jew wrong a Christian, what is his humility? Revenge. If a Christian wrong a Jew, what should his sufferance be by Christian example? Why, revenge. The villany you teach me, I will execute, and it shall go hard but I will better the instruction.

Figure 3.1   Side-by-Side Comparison of Speeches from *A Raisin in the Sun* and *The Merchant of Venice*. Act III from *A Raisin in the Sun* by Lorraine Hansberry, copyright © 1958 by Robert Nemiroff, as an unpublished work. Copyright © 1959, 1966, 1984 by Robert Nemiroff. Copyright renewed 1986, 1987 by Robert Nemiroff. Used by permission of Random House, an imprint and division of Penguin Random House LLC. All rights reserved.

ACTIVITY THREE: SYNTACTICAL OTHERING

It must appear in other ways than words.[4]

Yet another intertextual connection between these two plays is the extent to which, in each play, Otherness is achieved syntactically—through the choice and arrangement of words.

In the following scene from Act II, Scene 3 of *A Raisin in the Sun*, Mr. Lindner is warming up to the moment when he will tell the Younger family that they—or any other African American family—are not welcome in Clybourne Park.

Instruct students to read this scene closely, hunting for ways in which Lindner, while on the surface promoting goodwill, is defining the Youngers as "Others."

RUTH *(Still innocently) Would you like another chair—you don't look comfortable.*
LINDNER *(More frustrated than annoyed) No, thank you very much. Please. Well—to get right to the point I—(A great breath, and he is off at last) I am sure you people must be aware of some of the incidents which have happened in various parts of the city when colored people have moved into certain areas—(BENEATHA exhales heavily and starts tossing a piece of fruit up and down in the air) Well—because we have what I think is going to be a unique type of organization in American community life—not only do we deplore that kind of thing—but we are trying to do something about it. (BENEATHA stops tossing and turns with a new and quizzical interest to the man.) We feel—(gaining confidence in his mission because of the interest in the faces of the people he is talking to)—we feel that most of the trouble in this world, when you come right down to it—(He hits his knee for emphasis)—most of the trouble exists because people just don't sit down and talk to each other.*
    RUTH *(Nodding as she might in church, pleased with the remark)* You can say that again, mister.
LINDNER *(More encouraged by such affirmation) That we don't try hard enough in this world to understand the other fellow's problem. The other guy's point of view.*
RUTH *Now that's right. (BENEATHA and WALTER merely watch and listen with genuine interest.)*
LINDNER *Yes—that's the way we feel out in Clybourne Park. And that's why I was elected to come here this afternoon and talk to you people. Friendly like, you know, the way people should talk to each other and see if we couldn't find some way to work this thing out. As I say, the whole business is a matter of caring about the other fellow. Anybody can see that you are a nice family of folks, hardworking and honest I'm sure. (BENEATHA frowns slightly, quizzically, her head tilted regarding him.) Today everybody knows what it means to be on the outside of something. And of course, there is always somebody who is out to take advantage of people who don't always understand.*
WALTER *What do you mean?*[5]

By the end of this close reading activity, students should recognize that in his opening sentences, Lindner refers to the Youngers as "you people" before lumping them in more generally with "colored people." However, in the next two sentences, when talking about the Clybourne

Park Improvement Association, Lindner repeats the word "we" five times, creating a division between a first-person antecedent that includes Linder versus "you people." Lindner goes on then, in the guise of promoting communication, to repeat the word "other" five times before once again repeating "you people."

Therefore, Lindner's syntax has the effect of clearly establishing the Youngers as Other, setting up Lindner's attempt to buy back the home Lena Younger had just purchased.

Essentially, what Lindner is doing is making a pitch for tribalism disguised as a pitch for harmony.

Students can then compare this scene to a key scene from Act IV of *The Merchant of Venice*. In the climactic courtroom scene, when Shylock attempts to collect on his bond by taking a pound of flesh from Antonio's chest, Portia is brought in, disguised as a young doctor of law, to help decide the case.

A close reading of the scene reveals that Portia engages in syntactical Othering similar to that of Mr. Linder. Take her most famous speech, as an example:

The quality of mercy is not strained;
It droppeth as the gentle rain from heaven
Upon the place beneath. It is twice blest;
It blesseth him that gives and him that takes:
'T is mightiest in the mightiest; it becomes
The thronèd monarch better than his crown:
His sceptre shows the force of temporal power,
The attribute to awe and majesty,
Wherein doth sit the dread and fear of kings;
But mercy is above this sceptred sway;
It is enthronèd in the hearts of kings,
It is an attribute to God himself;
And earthly power doth then show likest God's
When mercy seasons justice. Therefore, Jew,
Though justice be thy plea, consider this,
That, in the course of justice, none of us
Should see salvation: we do pray for mercy;
And that same prayer doth teach us all to render
The deeds of mercy. I have spoke thus much
To mitigate the justice of thy plea;
Which if thou follow, this strict court of Venice
Must needs give sentence 'gainst the merchant there.[6]

Most of the speech consists of a series of metaphors personifying *mercy*—first as gentle, then as blessed, then as mighty, finally describing mercy as an attribute of not only kings but of God.

But following these lines, Portia goes on to distinguish between Shylock, the unmerciful *Other*, and merciful Christians, including herself in the latter group through the repeated use of *us* and *we*. The irony here is that Portia's *inclusion* is reliant on her male disguise; unbeknownst to the male Christians, she is the other *Other* in the room.

Furthermore, Portia's use of *we* and *us* contrasts with her referring to Shylock as "Jew," as she does eight other times in the scene, a word choice that simultaneously defines Shylock's identity and his Otherness and allows for, by the end of his scene, his humiliating undoing, just as Lindner's syntactical Othering of the Younger family paved the way for his denial of their right to live in the home of their choice.

ACTIVITY FOUR: WAS THERE A WAY AROUND THIS?

What you just said about the circle. It isn't a circle—it is simply a long line—as in geometry, you know, one that reaches into infinity. And because we cannot see the end—we also cannot see how it changes.[7]

What if students, after encountering both texts, could hypothetically re-enter the text? What if they could consider what the laws and policies were, what the implicit (or explicit) cost of those policies were for characters in the text, and what if they could rewrite those policies and reflect on how that would have changed the play?

Think of this activity as a model United Nations type of exercise. Students understand the players, the needs, the structure, and then they become empowered to discover a path forward that makes sense.

Students would have already encountered data and research on the practice of redlining in America. Students would have been introduced to the idea of mandated "ghettos" of Renaissance Venice. They'll know about the wage gap for Black Americans, and the limited professions available for Jews in Venice.

Challenge them with a simple (yet sophisticated) prompt: What in society would need to be different? What changes in policy and legislation would need to be in place to change the tragedies in each of these plays? If both share a thread of the cost of systems that promote (nay, insist) on socio-economic inequality, what is needed in those systems and how would those changes affect the story?

Students could be placed in teams, and challenged to present the most realistic ideas to a panel; the panel itself could also be made up of students.

Each team would present their research and their proposals, and the panel would consider each, and choose the winner. The panel would be graded on their evaluation skills of each plan, and the teams would be graded on their research and logic.

At the end of such an immersive task, students should write a reflection: can policies produce human tragedy?

CONCLUSION

Certainly there are other similarities between these two texts. Comparing and contrasting power dynamics or gender roles (among many other things) would all provide ample opportunity for analytical comparison. Ultimately, however, what we learn by pairing seemingly different texts is the universality of our shared experiences.

When we begin with an issue—rather than a genre, specific theme, or author—we open up the possibilities in our classroom. In this chapter, we have demonstrated how the issue of socioeconomic injustice contributes to Othering, and how these systemic issues of inequality—despite time and place—exact a price that is too high to pay on the individual and the society.

Don't be afraid to make odd choices in pairing works intertextually. Let the issue resonate across units, let students wrestle with it, recognize it, respect it, and, hopefully, begin to glimpse a way through it.

NOTES

1. Lorraine Hansberry, *A Raisin in the Sun* (New York, NY: Vintage Books, 2004), 140.

2. Lorraine Hansberry, *To Be Young, Gifted and Black* (New York, NY: Signet NAL, 1979).

3. William Shakespeare, *The Merchant of Venice*, ed. Barbara A. Mowat and Paul Werstine (New York, NY: Simon & Schuster Paperbacks, 2011).

4. Shakespeare, *The Merchant of Venice*, 198.

5. Hansberry, *A Raisin in the Sun*, 116–17.

6. Shakespeare, *The Merchant of Venice*, 164–6.

7. Hansberry, *A Raisin in the Sun*, 134.

Chapter 4

Abuses of Power in *One Flew Over the Cuckoo's Nest*

Reading *One Flew Over the Cuckoo's Nest* by Ken Kesey is always an emotional experience. There is something so hopeful in it that lasts so long that it seems truly possible that the world will right itself, and justice will have its day. It almost happens. But what happens instead is a horror story.

Horror stories, in either narrative or film, are particularly effective because they allow us to recognize the vulnerability of our situations. Rarely are such stories anchored to people who bring such events upon themselves; rather, they are effective because normal people are thrust into untenable situations. Therein lies the horror. It was them this time, but next time it could be us.

Kesey's *Cuckoo's Nest* forces us to examine how precarious our personhood is; how merely a shift in setting or a change in power dynamics can shift us away from a moment of terror into a life of horror.

It does this by examining a situation in which society gets to decide what happens to a person. If a person is, for instance, "crazy"—if society *says* a person is "crazy," then that person becomes a problem to be solved by those who are "able" to solve it. The same syntactical stigma could apply to a myriad of subgroups of society. Insert "prisoner," for instance, or "criminal." The problem arises when we recognize that not all people granted such power to decide what happens to these groups can be trusted. And that's where the horror starts.

In this chapter, we will investigate the power of power. Does it innately corrupt? Does a little power go too far? Why do we obey everyday tyrants like Nurse Ratched? Why are so many of us rabbits? And what is the cost of standing up to wolves?

ACTIVITY ONE: AN UNCOMFORTABLE QUICKWRITE

I been silent so long now it's gonna roar out of me like floodwaters and you think the guy telling this is ranting and raving my God; you think this is too horrible to have really happened, this is too awful to be the truth! But, please. It's still hard for me to have a clear mind thinking on it. But it's the truth even if it didn't happen.[1]

To begin this text, take the opportunity to demonstrate how power (and abuses of power) is not only found in extreme settings like insane asylums. Your students, too, have probably been privy to some variation of a McMurphy/Ratched battle of wills.

Ask students to think about a time they saw someone abuse their power. Maybe it was obvious. Maybe it had consequences. Or maybe it didn't. Have students think of a person in power they may know (a teacher, a coach, etc.) someone who had a degree of power over them and their peers. Have you ever seen such a person "hunt" someone they are in charge of? For instance, students tend to know when teachers dislike a particular student. They have all witnessed it.

Next, have them reflect on what was done about it. 99 out of 100 times, the answer is nothing. There was nothing to do, exactly, because nothing explicitly wrong had been done. So everyone knows there is an abuse of power, without being able to prove it.

But it's the truth, even if it didn't (probably) happen.

This chapter does not seek to suggest that mental illness is merely a syntactical exercise. An entire book could be devoted (and there are several that are) to young people navigating the mental health crisis in this country. Rather, this chapter looks at a novel that happens to be set in a location where the installed power structure gets to bandy about words like "insane," and this setting works as a metaphor for power dynamics that are, perhaps, unjust. Society still has pockets where a label can, potentially, disenfranchise a person. The right word applied to a person can result in their loss of power. "Resisting arrest," for instance. Or someone in power "fears for their life."

This seems particularly true when disenfranchised people get angry. Your students may be familiar with the term "gaslighting." Here, we will consider the extreme of gaslighting. What is the correlation between being mad (a word that, interestingly, means both anger *and* insanity) about something, and being treated like you're dangerous? Crazy? Threatening? When did that false equivalency become part of our culture? And what are we risking if we continue to enable it?

Why Do Societies Kill Their Heroes?

Let us begin with an exploration about what it is about heroes (in life and in literature) that seems to result in so many of them being murdered. What is the correlation between standing up for the little guy and being seen as a threat that must be put down?

Cuckoo's Nest is incredibly moving, in part, because a downtrodden cast of characters are given back their personhood by our (problematic and unlikely) hero, R.P. McMurphy. We know he's going to die as soon as we meet him. His tattoo of "aces and eights" indicates that—just like his historical antecedent, Wild Bill Hickok—he's been dealt a dead man's hand. The foreshadowing is heavy throughout.

Added onto this are the obvious literary parallels between McMurphy and Jesus Christ. Mac "resurrects" the patients' personhoods, he "baptizes" them with laughter on the boat trip, he is "crucified" during Electroconvulsive Therapy (ECT)—the correlations are everywhere.

But what the text asks is even more complicated: What is the cost of being a hero? Consider the following passage. Heroes, though perhaps remembered in the history books, rarely live lives of calm and peace. They walk into the fire for those who can't, as McMurphy does for the patients. Have students annotate this passage from near the end of the novel and consider why McMurphy's character arc end as it does. Ultimately, with a passage like this, Kesey seems to have his audience wonder (via his first-person narration of chief) whether or not it was worth it.

> *First I had a quick thought to try to stop him, talk him into taking what he'd already won and let her have the last round, but another, bigger thought wiped the first thought away completely. I suddenly realized with a crystal certainty that neither I nor any of the half-score of us could stop him. That Harding's arguing or my grabbing him from behind, or old Colonel Matterson's teaching or Scanlon's griping, or all of us together couldn't rise up and stop him. We couldn't stop him because we were the ones making him do it. It wasn't the nurse that was forcing him, it was our need that was making him push himself slowly up from sitting, his big hands driving down on the leather chair arms, pushing him up, rising and standing like one of those moving-picture zombies, obeying orders beamed at him from forty masters.*
>
> *It was us that had been making him go on for weeks, keeping him standing long after his feet and legs had given out, weeks of making him wink and grin and laugh and go on with his act long after his humor had been parched dry between two electrodes. We made him stand and hitch up his black shorts like they were horsehide chaps, and push back his cap with one finger like it was a ten-gallon Stetson, slow, mechanical gestures—and when he walked across the floor you could hear the iron in his bare heels ring sparks out of the tile. Only at the last—after he'd smashed through that glass door, her face swinging around, with terror forever ruining any other look she might ever try to use again, [. . .] only then did he show any sign that he might be anything other*

than a sane, willful, dogged man performing a hard duty that finally just had to be done, like it or not.

He gave a cry. At the last, falling backward, his face appearing to us for a second upside down before he was smothered on the floor by a pile of white uniforms, he let himself cry out: A sound of cornered-animal fear and hate and surrendered defiance, that if you ever trailed coon or cougar or lynx is like the last sound the treed and shot and falling animal makes as the dogs get him, when he finally doesn't care any more about anything but himself and his dying.[2]

There's a purposeful lack of heroics, here, certainly. Rather, the audience is forced to recognize that Mac, by taking on Big Nurse, is sacrificing himself for others and that he is exhausted and scared. Mac never speaks again and goes offstage until he re-enters as a lobotomy victim. His sacrifice correlates with the men finding their righteous anger and their dignity; many on the ward have left, and none are afraid of Big Nurse anymore. But was it worth it? Why does society—too often—kill their heroes?

ACTIVITY TWO: RESEARCHING ASSASSINATED HEROES

He was in his chair in the corner, resting a second before he came out for the next round—in a long line of next rounds. The thing he was fighting, you couldn't whip it for good. All you could do was keep on whipping it, till you couldn't come out anymore and somebody else had to take your place.[3]

With the passage from the previous activity in mind, and any other moments in the text (and there are many), have students write an expository piece of writing that asks the following question: Using Kesey's *One Flew Over the Cuckoo's Nest* and any applicable nonfiction texts, what, in your opinion, is the cost of being a hero? And, in your opinion, is it worth it?

Instruct students to support their answer with well-chosen embedded textual evidence. And, for a nonfiction research opportunity, consider the following process:

Have students explore the correlation between a person being angry at injustice and being perceived as a threat—so much so that lives have been taken. Students can pair up and research one of the following assassinated heroes. They should look for their major achievements and/or goals, their public perception, and details of how and why they were killed:

1. Abraham Lincoln
2. John F. Kennedy

3. Robert F. Kennedy
4. Martin Luther King, Jr.
5. Malcolm X
6. John Lennon
7. Mahatma Gandhi
8. Medgar Evers

Please add on any other heroic person you would like.

For instance, consider giving students the following article about the assassination of Civil Rights leader, Medgar Evers, and discussing the following questions: What was it that Evers represented? What was he fighting for that seemed so dangerously crazy to someone else, that they would kill to stop it?

• "Byron De La Beckwith, 80, Dies," *The Washington Post*, January 23, 2001.

The article is an obituary for Evers's killer, Byron De La Beckwith. In the article, Beckwith is quoted, as an explanation of the killing, as stating that he was "willing to kill the evil in this country that would try to push [him] out."[4]

Have students present the findings of their research into assassinated heroes. Then, as a whole group, facilitate a conversation about any similarities between all of these tragedies. What was it about standing up that correlated with someone shooting them down?

What do these correlations between the above people suggest about our predisposition to killing our societal rabble-rousers? And in what ways does Kesey foreshadow McMurphy's death with direct consideration of this conversation? How is he characterized as a hero for the masses?

ACTIVITY THREE: THE RIGHTEOUSNESS OF ANGER

Here; all you guys. What the hell is the matter with you? You ain't as crazy as all this, thinking you're some animal.[5]

One similarity that may apply to many of the names listed above is that they expressed anger and disbelief at the injustice around the world. In short, there was righteousness to their anger.

Ask your students what their relationship to anger is. When they reflect back on their childhoods, what were they implicitly and explicitly taught about anger? What were they *ever* taught about it? How did their childhood media attempt to prevent them from expressing it? In other words, think of *all* the stuff for kids that are about "calmly expressing yourself" and "behaving." Obviously, those are important lessons, but one unintended consequence of that messaging is that it may lead children to the perhaps unhealthy belief that anger is always bad.

When really, in life, there is plenty to be angry about.

Consider having students read the following article about the necessity of anger in their lives:

• "The Simple Truth about Anger" by Robert W. Firestone, Ph.D. *Psychology Today,* October 28, 2014.[6]

This is a great opportunity to have students start annotating an unfamiliar nonfiction text. Have them look for main ideas, concrete details, and applicable textual evidence. Beyond that, have them compare this research with their own lessons or inherent understanding about anger. Did the research support what they were taught, or was it counter to it?

McMurphy works as a hero because, in part, he convinces the men they are being mistreated, and that they have the right to get angry about it. He convinces them that there is injustice on the ward and that their anger is righteous.

And, of course, he is killed for it.

What is it about righteous anger that society finds so threatening? Obviously, we shouldn't strangle people, even when they are behaving as villains in our lives. Obviously, McMurphy is wrong in his behavior. There's a lot wrong with this text.

Nevertheless, embed time for students to write a reflection about the text's relationship to anger. Where does the text start with it, and where does it end? Can anger ever be redemptive? Can it ever be necessary? Why were some people so angry at the above list of heroes that they could kill them?

A Book about Stigmas and Their Power

As an American novel, *One Flew Over the Cuckoo's Nest* is a book that knows the heritage of American storytelling. It knows that so many of our texts rely on the myth of a hero being able to swim, and a loser sinking beneath pressure. Our narratology relies on these heroes: Huck and the brave act of shunning societal pressure, Ishmael (talk about unreliable narrators) being the lone survivor, Hester Prynne standing atop that scaffold, defiant of the world's expectations. This is our legacy. We are believers in the idea that there are winners and losers in life.

What is so compelling about this text is that it begins with a cast of characters society has already determined to be losers, sinkers, and the sunk. To begin a story within an insane asylum wherein every single person has been unable to function in society is a wonderful conceit. We are not supposed to root for these people.

What Kesey's novel manages to do is to grant the sunken among us their dignity. Because it is not the story of the fall of these characters, but rather what happens after they have long since fallen, we see the absolute necessity of reconsidering how we treat those least among us.

Another quintessential American text, *Death of a Salesman*, includes a moment that clarifies this. When Linda Loman finally erupts at her two sons who were so embarrassed by their father, she draws attention to what America does to those who haven't reached any greatness in their lives: "I don't say he's a great man. Willy Loman never made a lot of money. His name was never in the paper. He's not the finest character that ever lived. But he's a human being, and a terrible thing is happening to him. So attention must be paid. He's not to be allowed to fall into his grave like an old dog. Attention, attention must be finally paid to such a person."[7]

Kesey seems to have recognized the moral imperative we have to examine how we discard those among us who are unable to make the cut.

How, the text asks, do we pay attention to those who have failed our sink or swim test? How do we treat the losers in society? And, more dangerous, *why* do we do that? Why does society try so hard to label and distance themselves from anyone who is different from what they are supposed to be?

This is a book that forces us to reconsider the cheap and easy labels we use. What is good? What is right? What is sane? And are these territories vastly different from their opposites? Can something be called "crazy" long enough that it actually becomes insane? Can enough societal power deem what is good and what is bad? Do these things exist in intangible certainty, or are they constructs we create as a society because they make us feel better?

Power, Power Everywhere, and Nary a Drop to Drink

Cuckoo's Nest is certainly a text that suggests a correlation between feeling powerless in one's life and feeling crazy. The extent to which that correlation is true is certainly up for debate, but what the premise allows is an appreciation of how fighting power can often lead society to label those rebelling as "trouble-makers." Consider one of the opening passages, in which we come to understand *a lot* about Big Nurse, her power, the power of labeling, and the consequences of disobedience in this setting:

> *The guys file by and get a capsule in a paper cup—throw it to the back of the throat and get the cup filled with water by the little nurse and wash the capsule down.*
>
> *On rare occasions some fool might ask what he's being required to swallow.*

*"Wait just a shake, honey; what are these two little red capsules in here with
my vitamin?" I know him. He's a big, griping Acute, already getting the reputa-
tion of being a troublemaker.*

"It's just medication, Mr. Taber, good for you. Down it goes, now."

"But I mean what kind of medication. Christ, I can see that they're pills —"

*"Just swallow it all, shall we, Mr. Taber—just for me?" She takes a quick
look at the Big Nurse to see how the little flirting technique she is using is
accepted, then looks back at the Acute. He still isn't ready to swallow something
he don't know what is, not even just for her.*

*"Miss, I don't like to create trouble. But I don't like to swallow something
without knowing what it is, neither. How do I know this isn't one of those funny
pills that makes me something I'm not?"*

"Don't get upset, Mr. Taber —"

"Upset? All I want to know, for the lova Jesus —"

*But the Big Nurse has come up quietly, locked her hand on his arm, paralyzes
him all the way to the shoulder. "That's all right, Miss Flinn," she says. "If Mr.
Taber chooses to act like a child, he may have to be treated as such. We've tried
to be kind and considerate with him. Obviously, that's not the answer. Hostility,
hostility, that's the thanks we get. You can go, Mr. Taber, if you don't wish to
take your medication orally."*[8]

Have students work with this passage. If they were to do an analytical
close-read of it, what could be surmised? Some things that may come up:

- Those with power (the assistant and Big Nurse) condescend to Mr. Taber.
  They "Other" him.
- They are giving him a reason to get angry, and yet behaving as if to be
  angry is a sign of insanity.
- There is a threat implicit in Ratched's response; if he doesn't obey, she has
  the power to force him into a worse position—this abuse of power is within
  her rights, but is still wrong.
- Losing one's dignity is crazy-making.

This book is so powerful, because it picks up where *Hamlet* leaves off.
Everyone in Elsinore treats Hamlet as if he's insane. But because of his
position as an intellectual and a prince, though we recognize the indig-
nity of this, and the vulnerability of this, Hamlet has enough power and
autonomy to mock what is happening to him ("these tedious old fools"). But
Mr. Taber in *Cuckoo's Nest* can do no such thing. Society has deemed him
crazy, and thus, he has had his rights to dignity and information stripped
from him.

Chief Bromden doesn't tell us the above anecdote to prepare the audience for the heroics that are in store; no. He tells us the above as a warning.
Making trouble will get you called crazy. It is dangerous to make a move.

GODS AND MONSTERS, WHALES AND MEN: DOES POWER INNATELY CORRUPT?

Big Nurse is known for her absolute power on the ward. What she accomplishes with the "rabbiting" of the men is a result of her control over them. They need her for privileges, and they need her for their success or failure on the ward.

She is utterly in control until the force of nature (and perhaps entirely hallucinated) R.P. McMurphy shows up, willing to risk it all to take on her abuses of power. It's no mistake the novel leans so heavily on *Moby Dick* and allusions to Jesus Christ and his apostles. The idea Kesey suggests is this: people are so susceptible to the draw of power; it is so ubiquitous, it would take an act of God, or some mythological force to topple what seems so utterly in control all around us, all the time. It takes a clash of two titans, a white whale pitted against Ahab, to see if decency can be truly restored.

Activity Four: Analyzing Allusions

I think for a fact that she'd rather he'd of been stark naked under that towel than had on those shorts. She's glaring at those big white whales leaping round on his shorts in pure wordless outrage.[9]

In small groups, assign students an allusion used in the text. Groups will research the origins of this allusion, and prepare a presentation examining both the history of the allusion and what the heck it is doing in this particular novel.

Does Kesey rely on the allusion to characterize people? Or to foreshadow what will inevitably happen? Does the allusion help demonstrate the mythical struggles taking place? Or does it symbolize the power struggle between Big Nurse and McMurphy? What is the purpose of these authorial choices, and why must the audience understand and appreciate these choices in order to appreciate the goal of the text?

BIG NURSE: POSSIBLY THE BEST ANTAGONIST IN THE LAST 100 YEARS

Nurse Ratched never does anything wrong. She has a job, and she is succeeding at it. She is polite, on-task, well-mannered. And yet, from the perspective of those whom she is controlling, we recognize the sadism of her character. Mac fights to the death; her method is death by a thousand cuts. Nothing can actually be traced back to her directly.

And that is why she is so familiar. And infuriating.

It's interesting to note, perhaps, that the novel presents Nurse Ratched as our antagonist, most definitely. She is our alluded-to Ahab, unjustly trying to reign in the righteous nature of our whale-wearing McMurphy.

But Nurse Ratched is, essentially, middle management. She holds very little power outside that ward. Now, as many of us who have had obnoxious bosses know, sometimes a little power goes a long way toward empowering awful people. It doesn't take much to become drunk on one's own power.

But anyone outside the ward would have every reason to think *she* was the hero. She is the hardworking, longsuffering nurse, devoted to her patients. She's the one strangled at the end.

This consideration is important to note, in part, because we must acknowledge both sides have the ability to spin their heroics. Byron De La Beckwith shot a husband, father, and Civil Rights leader in the back, and thought he was acting heroically, because no one was going to "push him out." It's a safe bet that there were plenty of people who agreed with his actions.

Which is all to say, part of the power of *Cuckoo's Nest* is that it tells a story of power from the point of view of the powerless men on the ward. This choice shows us anyone can act a hero, or cast themselves as a hero. That's not the same as being one.

This is why, to a literature junky, Big Nurse is so incredibly effective. We all know her. We have all met some iteration of her. You can't prove she's doing anything malicious, but powerless people witnessing the wielding of her power know exactly what she is doing. Who needs a twirling mustache when we see what is so obviously effective—and deniable?

We want students thinking about this text as an example of what power has the ability to do. We want them considering how power can be a corrupting force and so easily abused when paired with particularly powerless populations.

This begs the question, then, what can we do as individuals in the face of such an abuse of power? This question could, perhaps, be considered as a culminating assessment. In the face of an abuse of power, what is our civic duty? Our ethical duty? Our personal duty? And is it worth it?

ACTIVITY FIVE: ARE WE HARDWIRED TO OBEY?

Oh, don't misunderstand me, we're not in here because we are rabbits—we'd be rabbits wherever we were—we're all in here because we can't adjust to our rabbithood. We need a good strong wolf like the nurse to teach us our place.[10]

Have students read the following three articles. The first provides an overview of what power does to the brain. The second gives an overview of the Stanford Prison Experiment, wherein a group of peers was divided into two groups: one group had power, because they were cast as the prison guards, and the other group did not, because they were cast as prisoners. The third discusses Stanley Milgrim's experiments on torture and obedience, and questions why (particularly well-behaved, agreeable) people will obey an unjust order.

Have students annotate each article, and then present correlations they find between these articles, real-life events they can point to (perhaps from their research on assassinated heroes) and *Cuckoo's Nest.* How can this activity that relies on intertextuality shed light on people's dubious relationship with power?

Article 1

• "What Power Does to Your Brain and Your Body" by Hilary Brueck, *Business Insider,* December 15, 2017.[11]

In this first article, students will encounter the physiological and psychological results of power. What does it actually do to us that makes us behave so poorly? How can we protect ourselves from succumbing to power's influence?

Article 2

• "Stanford Prison Experiment" by the Editors of *Encyclopedia Britannica,* last updated May 5, 2020.[12]

This article gives a solid overview of the experiment, with which students may not already be familiar. Have them pay particular attention to the randomness of the roles given and how the experiment quickly unraveled.

Article 3

• "The Psychology of Torture" by Malcom Harris, *Aeon.*[13]

This article does a good job providing a context for the Stanford Prison Experiment, particularly Milgrim's main goal: trying to figure out how thousands of Nazis could comply with those monstrous orders. What, Milgrim wanted to know, was it about humans that made them overly ready—nay, even anxious, to obey?

All of these articles beg the question of our students: what should we do if something is wrong? At what point (if any) is disobeying an order the right thing to do? And why do we find it so hard? As an individual? As a society? Further, if we know these issues exist, what can we do to safeguard ourselves from mindlessly following an unworthy power structure? Can a society be safeguarded against such a thing?

For the final assessment, have students reflect on their learning, and choose which direction they are most interested in exploring further.

Final Essay

Instructions: Choose one of the prompts below, and construct a three- to five-page research paper that is analytical in nature:

1. In what ways is this a text about freedom versus confinement?
2. In what ways is this a text about the righteousness of anger?
3. In what ways is this a misogynistic text?
4. Discuss power dynamics within the novel.
5. To what extent do allusions parallel the plot of the novel?
6. In what ways does McMurphy serve as a Christ archetype?
7. Why is it important to our understanding of the text that this is from the POV of an unreliable narrator?
8. What does this text ultimately say about sanity versus insanity?
9. Discuss the significance of animal imagery in the text.
10. What does this text suggest is the correlation between powerlessness and insanity?

Sample Student Essay

The following is a sample essay written by an eleventh grade student in response to response number 6 above.

McMurphy and Martyrdom

In Ken Kesey's One Flew Over the Cuckoo's Nest, *the character R.P. McMurphy is the Christ archetype for the patients being controlled in Nurse Ratched's psychiatric ward. McMurphy and Ratched are polar opposite characters, McMurphy being completely based off of instincts, filled with righteous anger, sexually free, and representing an unconquerable force of nature while Nurse Ratched is controlling, emasculates the patients, and represents the "machine" of the text. Their feud ultimately shows the struggle between their ways of exerting power in the ward, both characters manipulating the system to gain what they want and countering each other in every way. However, Nurse Ratched, being the "machine," wins due to her place in the power structure and McMurphy loses his life through his anger. This does not go without purpose: McMurphy serving as the martyr allows for the healing of the other patients, inspiring them, and weakens the control Ratched has over them.*

McMurphy initially is not a character that fits the role of a Christ figure. In fact, he chooses to fake insanity to be allowed into the ward to escape work from criminal charges. When he enters the ward, he is introduced as a drinking, gambling, boisterous person with a zest for women and wanting to have a good time. These characteristics belong to a Dionysian archetype rather than those of a Christ archetype. However, as McMurphy gets to know the other patients, he begins to shift towards said figure. For example, after the first group meeting, McMurphy questions why they let Nurse Ratched make them endure a "pecking party" and does not like the answer Harding gives him: they are "rabbits" that need help from the "wolf" to accept their "rabbit" roles.

This suggests a character not fooled by Ratched's subtle condescending manner and someone who wants to change the power structure. This is important because McMurphy does this because he sees how Ratched is treating the others, making them feel like "rabbits," and uses a bet to challenge the "machine." Through Part I, McMurphy's acts of righteousness begin to change the other patients' behaviors. When McMurphy tries to change the ward policy for the television for the World Series and no one backs him up, he exemplifies his efforts by attempting to lift an impossibly heavy control panel. Although he fails, the other members believed for a second that he could overthrow the machine.

This is important because the panel is a metaphor for Nurse Ratched's control and this situation compels them to try and resist her. The other patients eventually do go against the Big Nurse and vote for the World Series despite the risk. When she does not count Chief's vote and let them watch the game, McMurphy leads a protest along with other patients that join him by watching the blank TV screen. This leads to Nurse Ratched falling apart, screaming and ordering the patients to return to their work, and McMurphy to win the bet. This is important because McMurphy leads his twelve "disciples" to challenge unfairness, control, and make strides for righteousness. As the story of the ward furthers, it is clear that McMurphy is an extended metaphor for Jesus Christ.

However, through his resistance and the resurrection of the patients, McMurphy allows himself to become a "walking target" for Nurse Ratched. For example, at the fishing trip, all the men are struggling to catch a fish and McMurphy just laughs at them. This event parallels with the fishing trip Jesus takes his twelve disciples on. Furthermore, McMurphy's laugh is a symbol of natural forces (in comparison to nurse Ratched's machine) and salvation for the men. This is important because through this lesson, McMurphy teaches the men to be independent, brave, and carry his morals without his direct help. However, after this trip, McMurphy looked "so beat and worn out" and "dreadfully tired and strained."

This metaphorically compares to the last days of Jesus and how tired he was serving those on earth for the will of God. This is important because as McMurphy battles the machine, he slowly and surely is being destroyed in the process while the other men are empowered by his actions. Finally, after the night of all the patients partying (which parallels with the Last Supper) McMurphy attacks Nurse Ratched after she shames Billy, who commits suicide because he is once more emasculated by the Nurse and betrays McMurphy. McMurphy acknowledges that he has an opportunity to leave and knows that attacking Nurse Ratched assures certain death; however, McMurphy does so anyways to finish his path of righteousness. Through his death he lives on as a free spirit and an inspiring symbol for someone who stood up against the power structure.

Kesey's novel uses McMurphy as the Christ figure while Nurse Ratched serves as the Antichrist. Through their feud for power, McMurphy sacrifices himself to the "machine" for the sake of other patients through his disobedience and defiance of the authority. Though he is lobotomized, Chief killing him allows him to beat the machine: he is not used as a cautionary tale for other patients but rather a story and symbol for others to revolt against Nurse Ratched. His martyrdom allows him to escape the wrath of the machine, inspiring strength in others, and employing them to follow in his path.

CONCLUSION

Hopefully, by the end of the unit, students have an appreciation for how power can corrupt. They will have reflected on their own upbringing and its implicit (or explicit) messages about anger, and their own passivity in the face of injustice. Additionally, they will have had half a dozen research opportunities to explore how societies can become so prone to obeying unjust mandates.

They will have studied a dynamic and compelling piece of literature, and within its pages, discovered their own part in power dynamics all around them, while also understanding global and historical ramifications of these same basic principles.

Finally, they will have been given the opportunity to thoughtfully consider the cost of being a hero, and how a hero risks the wrath of those unwilling to accept righteous anger that disrupts a corrupted (and empowered) status quo.

NOTES

1. Ken Kesey, *One Flew Over the Cuckoo's Nest* (New York, NY: Berkley, an imprint of Penguin Random House LLC, 2016), 13.

2. Kesey, *One Flew Over the Cuckoo's Nest*, 266–7.

3. Kesey, *One Flew Over the Cuckoo's Nest*, 265.

4. "Byron De La Beckwith, 80, Dies," The Washington Post (WP Company, January 23, 2001), https://www.washingtonpost.com/archive/local/2001/01/23/byron-de-la-beckwith-80-dies/8f0599c3-f1f2-472d-9b94-960de04197fc/.

5. Kesey, *One Flew Over the Cuckoo's Nest*, 63.

6. Robert W Firestone, "The Simple Truth about Anger," Psychology Today (Sussex Publishers, October 28, 2014), https://www.psychologytoday.com/us/blog/the-human-experience/201410/the-simple-truth-about-anger.

7. Arthur Miller, *Death of a Salesman* (Oxford: Oxford University Press, 2019).

8. Kesey, *One Flew Over the Cuckoo's Nest*, 35.

9. Kesey, *One Flew Over the Cuckoo's Nest*, 90.

10. Kesey, *One Flew Over the Cuckoo's Nest*, 62.

11. Hilary Brueck, "What Power Does to Your Brain and Your Body," Business Insider (Business Insider, December 15, 2017), https://www.businessinsider.com/what-power-does-to-your-brain-and-your-body-2017-12.

12. The Editors of Encyclopaedia Britannica, "Stanford Prison Experiment," Encyclopædia Britannica (Encyclopædia Britannica, inc., May 5, 2020), https://www.britannica.com/event/Stanford-Prison-Experiment.

13. Malcolm Harris, "The Psychology of Torture," Aeon (Aeon, AD 7), https://aeon.co/essays/is-it-time-to-stop-doing-any-more-milgram-experiments.

Chapter 5

Authoritarianism in *1984* and *Animal Farm*

We have been teaching George Orwell's *1984* for about fifteen years, and, over the years, we've ended our units with a variety of culminating projects: a research paper, a debate, an original dystopian short story. All of these past projects were successful, but in the winter of 2018, shortly after the murder of the journalist Jamal Khashoggi, those previous assignments didn't seem sufficient. Authoritarianism and abuses of power were visibly on the rise around the world, and, as English teachers, the idea of not using George Orwell's fiction to illuminate and explore those abuses seemed like a dereliction of duty, particularly since Orwell's precise purpose was a warning against authoritarianism and totalitarianism.

This chapter will model a unit—with specific strategies and activities—designed to pair the rigorous, analytical, standards-based study of works of dystopian literature (in this case, *Animal Farm* and *1984*) and a real-time, research-based exploration of authoritarianism (including its methods and its consequences) in our world today.

DYSTOPIAN VOCABULARY

In order to be successful in this unit, students will need to be familiar with the following terms, which should be frontloaded:

1. Authoritarianism: a government in which the authority of a ruler is more important than the freedom of the people.
2. Communism: a government in which all goods and property is owned collectively by the people.

3. Fascism: a government in which a dictator has complete power and uses force to suppress opposition and criticism. Fascist dictators also often promote nationalism and racism.
4. Proletariat: the working class.
5. Propaganda: the intentional spreading of information (sometimes false) that benefits one group or person.
6. Totalitarianism: a government with total and absolute control over its citizens.

PAIRING *ANIMAL FARM* AND *1984*

George Orwell's most well-known books (certainly his most-*taught* books) are the two novels *Animal Farm* and *1984*, published in 1945 and 1949, respectively.

In many ways, they are two very different works. *Animal Farm* runs ninety pages (closer in length to a novella than a novel) and is set on a farm, and all of the characters are farm animals. *1984*, in contrast, is 300 pages of dark, dismal dystopia (with humans) set in a post-apocalyptic London, now the capital of the superstate, Oceania.

Despite these differences, Orwell explores the same themes—power, language, Otherness—and demonstrates the same issues of authoritarianism and propaganda.

Therefore, *Animal Farm*, given its length—it can be read rather quickly, whereas *1984* will take some time—makes for an effective introduction to *1984* and to abuse of power in our world today.

ALLEGORY OF THE RUSSIAN REVOLUTION

The ultimate purpose of this unit is to use fiction as an inroad to discussing real-time authoritarianism in the twenty-first century. That will come later. Our study of *Animal Farm* will focus on the twentieth century, specifically the Russian Revolution, of which *Animal Farm* is an *allegory*.

Students will need to be directly taught that an allegory is a work of literature (story, novel, poem, play) in which all of the elements, including the characters and events, are *symbols* representing real-world events (a definition that may be initially confusing to students, but which this short novel will quickly make clear).

Activity One: Researching the Russian Revolution

I do not know when that Rebellion will come, it might be a week or in a hundred years, but I know, as surely as I see this straw beneath my feet, that sooner or later justice will be done.[1]

The purpose of our study of *Animal Farm* is to answer the following question: To what extent is Orwell's *Animal Farm* an allegory of the Russian Revolution? Answering this question will require research on the events of the Russian Revolution. It may be the case that students have studied the revolution in their history class, or (better yet, though unlikely) they are studying it in history at the time that you are teaching this unit, but if neither is the case, students can conduct the necessary research as an activity in their English class.

If students are indeed researching the Russian Revolution in their English class, the following questions will guide students to the information they will need to answer the focus question: To what extent is George Orwell's *Animal Farm* an allegory of the Russian Revolution?:

Communist Manifesto
  ○ Who is Karl Marx? What is Marxism?
  ○ What is the Communist Manifesto?
  ○ What was the message of the Communist Manifesto?
Vladimir Lenin
  ○ Who is Vladimir Lenin?
  ○ What were Lenin's beliefs about the working class (aka proletariat)?
  ○ What role did Lenin play in the Russian Revolution?
Tsar Nicholas II
  ○ Who was Tsar Nicholas II?
  ○ What was life like in Russia during his rule?
  ○ What happens to him during the Russian Revolution?
Leon Trotsky
  ○ Who was Leon Trotsky?
  ○ What role did Trotsky play in the Russian Revolution?
  ○ How was Trotsky different from Joseph Stalin?
  ○ What happened to Trotsky after the Russian Revolution?
Joseph Stalin
  ○ Who was Joseph Stalin?
  ○ What was Stalin's role in the Russian Revolution?
  ○ How was Stalin different from Leon Trotsky?

○ How did Stalin use propaganda to gain power and remain in power?
○ How did Stalin use the KGB/secret police to gain power and remain in power?

Adolf Hitler
  ○ Who was Adolf Hitler?
  ○ What pact, or agreement, did Hitler make with the Soviet Union? Did he keep it?
  ○ How did Hitler use propaganda to gain power and remain in power?
  ○ How did Hitler use the Gestapo/secret police to gain power and remain in power?

These questions focus on specific *elements* of the Russian Revolution (mostly characters), all of which Orwell represents allegorically (mostly as farm animals) in *Animal Farm*.

PROPAGANDA: UNDERSTANDING POWER, LANGUAGE, AND OTHERNESS

The research questions above require students to explain specifically how Joseph Stalin and Adolf Hitler used propaganda both to gain power and to remain in power. Therefore, students need to understand what propaganda is and how it works. This understanding will help students to see the relationship between power, language, and Otherness.

In this unit, knowledge of propaganda will lead students, first, to recognize its use in the Russian Revolution and in *Animal Farm*, and, later, to recognize its use in *1984* and in the world today.

There are many types of propaganda, and students should know and understand as many as possible, but specific knowledge of the following types of propaganda will be useful to students over the course of this unit:

Propaganda Techniques

• Appeals to Fear: building support by causing anxiety or panic in the public.
• Pinpointing the Enemy: highlighting a common enemy that is the cause of all problems (so that the leaders are not criticized themselves).
• Ad Nauseam: A phrase or slogan that is repeated so often that the people believe it is true (or stop questioning its truth).
• Black-and-White Fallacy: Presenting only two choices; one is obviously better, and the other is terrible.

Activity Two: Propaganda Posters

When they had once got it by heart, the sheep developed a great liking for this maxim, and often as they lay in the field they would all start bleating "Four legs good, two legs bad! Four legs good, two legs bad!" and keep it up for hours on end, never growing tired of it.[2]

To assess and reinforce understanding of propaganda, assign groups of students one of the propaganda techniques listed above, along with poster paper and the following instructions:

Your poster must include:

- *An example from* Animal Farm *(cite page numbers),*
- *An example from the Russian Revolution (cite your source),*
- *A real-world example not from the Russian Revolution (cite your source).*

Animal Farm Essay

Before moving on to *1984,* students will write an essay on *Animal Farm* in response to the aforementioned focus question: To what extent is Orwell's *Animal Farm* an allegory for the Russian Revolution?

The following is a list of possible topics for the students' body paragraphs and guidelines for the format and content of their essay

- The rise of Communism (and fall of the Provisional Government)
- The conflict between Stalin and Trotsky
- Stalin's abuses of power (use of hard power/fear/violence to control citizens)
- Use of propaganda to control citizens
- The meaning of the novel's ending

Essay Guidelines

Introductory paragraph (two to five sentences—get in and get out)
- ○ Introduces the stories and the topic
- ○ Declares the thesis (what the essay will show or argue)

Three or more body paragraphs
- ○ Topic sentence that supports the thesis
- ○ Two to three specific supporting details, examples, quotations
- ○ Commentary/explanation of what the details demonstrate and how they support the thesis. These should not be obvious or repetitive (What does the detail imply? Why is it important?)
- ○ Transitional words and phrases that create a logical flow from one idea to the next

- ◦ Concluding sentence that reinforces the topic sentence/thesis and transitions to the next paragraph.

Concluding paragraph (two to five sentences—get in and get out)
  - ◦ Restate thesis in a new, fresh way
  - ◦ Summarize arguments presented in body paragraphs
  - ◦ Finish with a final, definitive, bold statement

Student Sample

The following is a sample essay from a tenth grade student:

Stalin's Abuse of Hard Power

George Orwell's Animal Farm *is considered an allegory as it uses various characters and events to represent the Russian Revolution. Napoleon the pig, for example, represents Joseph Stalin and his role in the Russian Revolution. Through Napoleon's character in the novel, Orwell demonstrates Joseph Stalin's abuses of power.*

To begin with, Napoleon's way of exiling Snowball with the dogs, parallels Stalin's approach to gaining power through brute force. Napoleon had the dogs chase Snowball "out of the door" in order to gain leadership over the animals in the barn. Like Napoleon, Stalin used military force to drive out his opponent, Leon Trotsky. This is important because Stalin abuses his military power in acts of terror to gain authority. In addition to this, animals who did not work on Sundays "would have his rations reduced by half." In order to get the animals to work for Napoleon, he used their food rations against them. This parallels to how Stalin used his hard power to benefit from the proletariat, without caring for their needs. By using the character Napoleon, Orwell shows Stalin's hard power through the dogs and how he benefits through the proletariat.

Furthermore, Stalin's abuse of power is shown through how Napoleon handles his opposition. Due to the hens' protest of laying eggs, Napoleon "ordered the hen's rations to be stopped . . . the dogs saw to it that these orders were carried out." Napoleon, like Stalin, abused his power and rid himself of threats against him. This event parallels to 1921 in which the sailors at the Kronshtadt military base attempted to rebel against Stalin, but ultimately failed. Moreover, the animals that confessed to crimes that opposed Napoleon, "were slain on the spot." In order to stay in power, Napoleon abuses his power to get rid of anyone who opposed him. This is similar to how Stalin brutally used the military to intimidate the citizens of Russia and maintain power. Napoleon's abuses correlate to how Stalin abused his power in order to continue to maintain leadership.

Additionally, Stalin's abuse of power is shown through how Napoleon puts the needs of the pigs above the need of the other animals. The leftover milk and apples that were missing were to be "reserved for the pigs alone" to keep the pigs in good health. By using Squealer, another pig that is a part of Napoleon's rule, Napoleon manages to justify the fact that he is taking advantage of the work of the animals to live a better carefree life. Napoleon's actions resemble Stalin and his approach to getting the benefits of being in power. Moreover, by the end of the novel, the commandments were changed to "ALL ANIMALS ARE EQUAL BUT SOME ARE MORE EQUAL THAN OTHERS." Napoleon changed the original commandments in order to clarify his importance above the other animals. In the same way Napoleon changed the commandments, Stalin used propaganda with his power to establish his importance over them whilst making it seem like it was the right thing to do. Orwell uses Napoleon's actions that abuse power, to resemble that of Joseph Stalin.

In Animal Farm *by George Orwell, characters and events are depicted to be an allegory to the Russian Revolution. By using the character Napoleon, Orwell symbolizes Joseph Stalin and his abuse of power.*

TRANSITIONING TO *1984*

As the unit transitions from *Animal Farm* to *1984*, students should apply what they have just learned about propaganda techniques and their effect. For example, students could complete an assignment like the following as they read the first chapter:

1984 Book One, Chapter 1
  ○ *Read Book One, Chapter I of 1984.*
  ○ *In notebook: write at least one page discussing the use of propaganda in Oceania. Focus on the following elements introduced in the chapter:*
    ○ *Victory Mansions*
    ○ *The poster*
    ○ *The three slogans of the party*
    ○ *Minitrue, Minipax, Miniluv, Miniplenty*
    ○ *The Two Minutes Hate*
    ○ *Goldstein*
    ○ *Big Brother*

All of the elements listed above are introduced in Book One, Chapter I, and each is an example of the types of propaganda also found in *Animal Farm,* particularly in that they represent an effort to maintain *power* through the use of *language*—sometimes with language that suggests *Otherness*.

Activity Three: Pairing Informational and Literary Texts

In its second minute the Hate rose to a frenzy.[3]

In the following activity, students will begin to make connections between propaganda and abuse of power in Orwell's fictional world with the abuse of power and propaganda in our world today.

Students are given three sources (two literary; one informational) and the following guiding questions:

- What techniques of propaganda are evident in each source, and what is the purpose of the use of propaganda in each source?
- What specific diction and/or imagery in Sources A and B support those purposes?
- Collectively, what do the three sources demonstrate about the power of propaganda and/or fear?

Source A: From *1984*, by George Orwell, Book
One, Chapter I (The Two Minutes Hate)

The next moment a hideous, grinding screech, as of some monstrous machine running without oil, burst from the big telescreen at the end of the room. It was a noise that set one's teeth on edge and bristled the hair at the back of one's neck. The Hate had started.

As usual, the face of Emmanuel Goldstein, the Enemy of the People, had flashed on to the screen. There were hisses here and there among the audience. The little sandy-haired woman gave a squeak of mingled fear and disgust. Goldstein was the renegade and backslider who once, long ago (how long ago, nobody quite remembered), had been one of the leading figures of the Party, almost on a level with Big Brother himself, and then had engaged in counter-revolutionary activities, had been condemned to death, and had mysteriously escaped and disappeared. The programmes of the Two Minutes Hate varied from day to day, but there was none in which Goldstein was not the principal figure. He was the primal traitor, the earliest defiler of the Party's purity. All subsequent crimes against the Party, all treacheries, acts of sabotage, heresies, deviations, sprang directly out of his teaching. Somewhere or other he was still alive and hatching his conspiracies: perhaps somewhere beyond the sea, under the protection of his foreign paymasters, perhaps even—so it was occasionally rumoured—in some hiding-place in Oceania itself.

Winston's diaphragm was constricted. He could never see the face of Goldstein without a painful mixture of emotions. It was a lean Jewish face, with a great fuzzy aureole of white hair and a small goatee beard—a clever face, and yet somehow inherently despicable, with a kind of senile silliness in the long thin nose near the end of which a pair of spectacles was perched. It resembled the face of a sheep, and the voice, too, had a sheeplike quality. [. . .] And all the while, lest one should be in any doubt as to the reality which Goldstein's specious claptrap covered, behind his head on the telescreen there marched the endless columns of the Eurasian army—row after row of solid-looking men with expressionless Asiatic faces, who swam up to the surface of the screen and vanished, to be replaced by others exactly similar. The dull rhythmic tramp of the soldiers' boots formed the background to Goldstein's bleating voice.

Before the Hate had proceeded for thirty seconds, uncontrollable exclamations of rage were breaking out from half the people in the room. The self-satisfied sheep-like face on the screen, and the terrifying power of the Eurasian army behind it, were too much to be borne: besides, the sight or even the thought of Goldstein produced fear and anger automatically.

In its second minute the Hate rose to a frenzy. People were leaping up and down in their places and shouting at the tops of their voices in an effort to drown the maddening bleating voice that came from the screen. [. . .]In a lucid moment Winston found that he was shouting with the others and kicking his heel violently against the rung of his chair. The horrible thing about the Two Minutes Hate was not that one was obliged to act a part, but, on the contrary, that it was impossible to avoid joining in. Within thirty seconds any pretence was always unnecessary. A hideous ecstasy of fear and vindictiveness, a desire to kill, to torture, to smash faces in with a sledge-hammer, seemed to flow through the whole group of people like an electric current, turning one even against one's will into a grimacing, screaming lunatic. And yet the rage that one felt was an abstract, undirected emotion which could be switched from one object to another like the flame of a blowlamp. Thus, at one moment Winston's hatred was not turned against Goldstein at all, but, on the contrary, against Big Brother, the Party, and the Thought Police; and at such moments his heart went out to the lonely, derided heretic on the screen, sole guardian of truth and sanity in a world of lies. And yet the very next instant he was at one with the people about him, and all that was said of Goldstein seemed to him to be true. At those moments his secret loathing of Big Brother changed into adoration, and Big Brother seemed to tower up, an invincible, fearless protector, standing like a rock against the hordes of Asia, and Goldstein, in spite of his isolation, his helplessness, and the doubt that hung about his very existence, seemed like some sinister enchanter, capable by the mere power of his voice of wrecking the structure of civilization.[4]

Source B: from *Animal Farm*, by George Orwell, Chapter VII

> *Presently the tumult died down. The four pigs waited, trembling, with guilt written on every line of their countenances. Napoleon now called upon them to confess their crimes. They were the same four pigs as had protested when Napoleon abolished the Sunday Meetings. Without any further prompting they confessed that they had been secretly in touch with Snowball ever since his expulsion, that they had collaborated with him in destroying the windmill, and that they had entered into an agreement with him to hand over Animal Farm to Mr. Frederick. They added that Snowball had privately admitted to them that he had been Jones's secret agent for years past. When they had finished their confession, the dogs promptly tore their throats out, and in a terrible voice Napoleon demanded whether any other animal had anything to confess.[5]*

Source C: "Turkey Issues a Warrant for Fethullah Gulen" by Ceylan Yeginsu, *The New York Times*, August 4, 2016[6]

This 2016 article describes the Turkish government's issuing of an arrest warrant for Fethullah Gulen. The warrant was issued after a failed coup attempt against Turkey's president, Recep Tayyip Erdogan (who is one of the potential topics of the Authoritarianism Research Project later in this chapter).

Gulen has lived in exile in Pennsylvania for decades, but Erdogan claims that Gulen orchestrated the coup and is the head of a terrorist organization. The article also describes how the Turkish government detained tens of thousands of individuals who the government claimed were aligned with Gulen.

Students should recognize, primarily, the use of "appeals to fear" and "pinpointing the enemy" in all of the above sources. In each example, one of which is real and contemporary, the oppressive government has identified a single individual as the "enemy of the people" and as the cause of all of the country's woes (and thereby to be feared above all else).

Students should also recognize, in the *1984* passage, the use of racial stereotypes to cast both Goldstein and the Eurasian Army as distinctly *foreign*, thereby associating their Otherness with the people's fear of them.

Each oppressive regime also uses this "enemy of the people" to justify violence against the regime's own citizens. In *Animal Farm*, for example, Napoleon coerces the pigs into confessing as conspirators with Snowball, then has them executed, using the fear of such an execution to maintain power over the masses. Similarly, Erdogan uses the 2016 coup attempt, which he alleges was orchestrated by Gulen, to justify the arrest of thousands of Turkish citizens.

As students make their way through *1984*, they will continually run head-on into the Party's use of propaganda techniques (specifically: appeals to fear, pinpointing the enemy, *ad nauseam*, black-and-white fallacy) in order to maintain power. Paying close attention to these examples will prepare students to make connections to contemporary events in the Authoritarianism Research Project described later in this chapter. More importantly, it will equip students to be aware when such techniques are targeting them.

ADDITIONAL FORMATIVE ACTIVITIES

Activity Four: Comrade Ogilvy and Wilbur S. Howard

It was true that there was no such person as Comrade Ogilvy, but a few lines of print and a couple of faked photographs would soon bring him into existence.[7]

Winston's job in the Ministry of Truth, ironically, is to fabricate lies. Specifically, his job is to alter past documents and newspaper articles so that they align with the lies (or propaganda) of the Party.

In Chapter IV of Book One, Winston received the task of "updating" a *London Times* article that mentions an individual that has been "vaporized" by the Party. Winston must invent an entirely new person, Comrade Ogilvy, to replace the vaporized "unperson." After doing so, Winston muses:

"Comrade Ogilvy, who had never existed in the present, now existed in the past, and when once the act of forgery was forgotten, he would exist just as authentically, and upon the same evidence, as Charlemagne or Julius Caesar."[8]

As a demonstration, invent a person yourself. In the past, we have used the name Wilbur S. Howard. We claimed that Howard was a Victorian poet who heavily influenced Orwell. Students took a full page of (made up) notes and analyzed a Howard poem (which was actually an excerpt from an Emily Dickinson poem).

Figures 5.1, 5.2, and 5.3 below represent the "notes" that students were given and the Dickinson excerpt, retitled and falsely attributed to the nonexistent Howard. After students had fully annotated the poem and participated in a lengthy class discussion on the poem's thematic connections to *1984*, we revealed that we had made all of it up.

Once their outrage subsided, we led a discussion that began with the question of whether or not Wilbur S. Howard exists. The answer was obviously no, but the next logical question was what evidence they have of the existence of, say, George Washington, and how that evidence differs from

Wilbur S. Howard (1874-1931)

-Political poet of Victorian Era

-Patronized by Queen Victoria for over 20 years
   -Speculation that he and Q.V. were romantically involved

-Never commercially successful, but highly regarded by the Queen and other writers (including Orwell)

Figure 5.1   "Notes" on Wilbur S. Howard.

Characteristics of Howard's Poetry:

-Relied heavily on emotionally distant observation of society
   -Nearly modernist in its emotional distance

-Usually brief (particularly for the time period)

-While covering the Spanish Civil War for the BBC, Orwell discovered and was influenced by Howard's poetry

-Many themes from Howard's poetry made their way into 1984

Figure 5.2   "Notes" on Wilbur S. Howard.

Read the following poem (one of Wilbur's most famous) and find thematic connections to 1984:

A Prison

A Prison gets to be a friend—
Between its Ponderous face
And Ours—a Kinsmanship express—
And in its narrow Eyes—

We come to look with gratitude
For the appointed Beam
It deal us—stated as our food—
And hungered for—the same—

We learn to know the Planks—
That answer to Our feet—
So miserable a sound—at first—
Nor ever now—so sweet—

   by Wilbur S. Howard (1916)

Figure 5.3   "Notes" on Wilbur S. Howard.

the evidence (such as a page of written notes) of the existence of Wilbur S. Howard.

Additionally, and no less important, is the idea that even in the *midst* of studying totalitarianism, students are still incredibly (frighteningly so, perhaps) willing to blindly accept the authority figure's word as to what is and is not real.

This activity forces students to question the information they are given, including the purpose of such information, perhaps making them more aware of and less susceptible to propaganda.

Activity Five: the Principles of Newspeak

It's a beautiful thing, the destruction of words.[9]

In Chapter V of Book One, Orwell introduces a character named Syme, whose job it is to eliminate words as the Party transitions from Oldspeak to Newspeak. Syme tells Winston that "the whole aim of Newspeak is to narrow the range of thought."[10]

In the back of *1984* is an Appendix titled "The Principles of Newspeak." Chapter V is an appropriate moment in the novel to turn to this appendix. In the past, we have synthesized the information in the appendix into a PowerPoint. Alternatively, you could assign groups of students to synthesize sections of the appendix to present to the class.

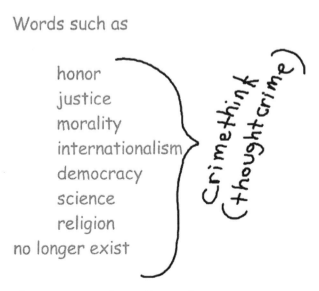

Figure 5.4   Classroom Presentation on Newspeak.

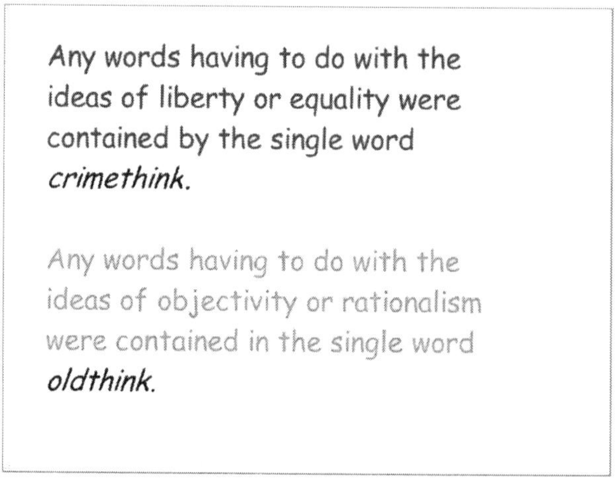

Any words having to do with the ideas of liberty or equality were contained by the single word *crimethink.*

Any words having to do with the ideas of objectivity or rationalism were contained in the single word *oldthink.*

Figure 5.5   Classroom Presentation on Newspeak.

The Newspeak Vocabulary grows smaller every year.

The fewer the choices in regards to words, the smaller the temptation and the ability to have a thought.

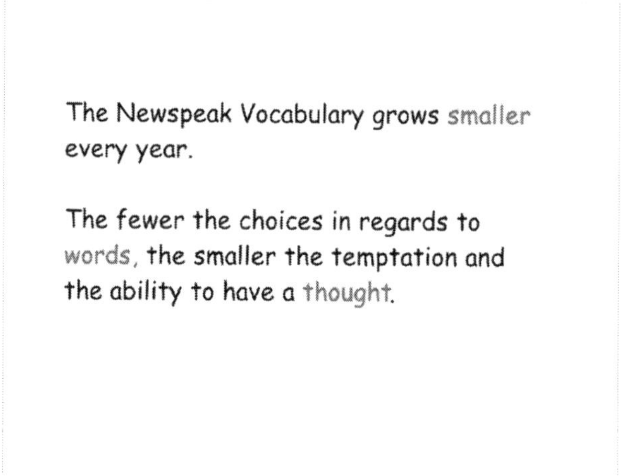

Figure 5.6   Classroom Presentation on Newspeak.

In either case, the goal is for students to understand *how* the Party will eliminate words, *why* the Party will benefit from such elimination, and *how* the elimination of words narrows "the range of thought."

Activity Six: 2 + 2= 5

In the end the Party would announce that two and two made five, and you would have to believe it.[11]

Early in the novel, Winston states that "*Freedom is the freedom to say that two plus two make four.*"[12] This may seem, to us, like a rather low bar, but in

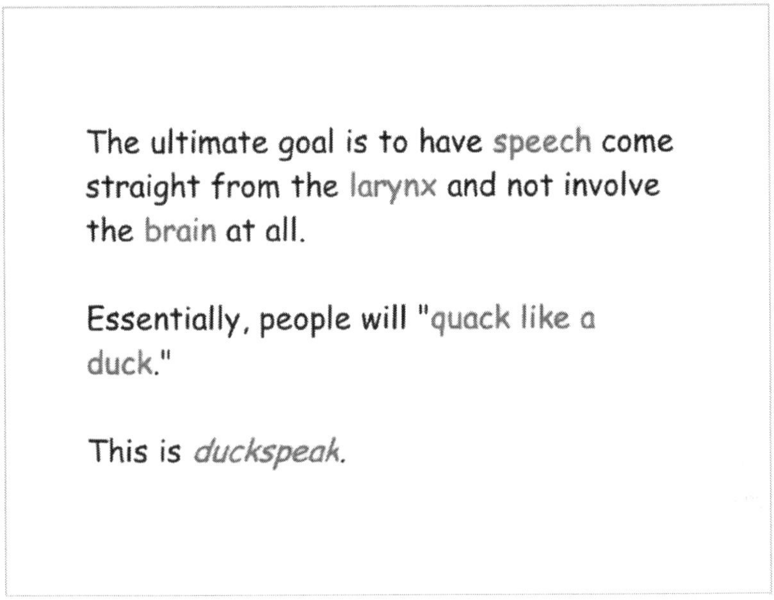

The ultimate goal is to have speech come straight from the larynx and not involve the brain at all.

Essentially, people will "quack like a duck."

This is *duckspeak*.

Figure 5.7   Classroom Presentation on Newspeak.

Book Three of the novel a central element of Winston's torture is O'Brien's insistence that Winston not only concede, but *believe*, that two plus two equals five.

As a demonstration, illicit the help of several students in the class. Speak to them secretly beforehand, and instruct them to behave in class as if $2 + 2 = 5$. Then, during class, find a moment to casually suggest that the sum of two and two is five. Some students may correct you, but your co-conspirators will back you.

If a majority of the class is insisting that $2+2 = 5$, and the minority has no idea what is going on, the activity is usually successful. The purpose of the activity is to demonstrate that "truth" or "facts" can be manipulated by those in power.

SUMMATIVE ACTIVITY: AUTHORITARIANISM RESEARCH PROJECT

The unit culminates with the Authoritarianism Research Project and the *1984* Final Essay, both of which focus on authoritarian leaders currently in power, in connection to Orwell's novel.

Assign groups of students one of the following current authoritarian leaders. Students will research their assigned leader/government and will prepare a ten-minute presentation that focuses on how these leaders gained power and how they have maintained power.

- Xi Jinping (China)
- Vladimir Putin (Russia)
- Kim Jong Un (North Korea)
- Bashar al-Assad (Syria)
- Rodrigo Duterte (Philippines)
- Abdel Fattah el-Sissi (Egypt)
- Recep Tayyip Erdogan (Turkey)
- Mohammed Bin Salman (Saudi Arabia)
- Nicolás Maduro (Venezuela)

The presentation should specifically focus on the following:

- Authoritarian governments are often ruled by a single party led by a dynamic leader (aka strong man). In some cases, this leader becomes a symbol for the nation.
- Authoritarian governments use terror and violence to force obedience and to crush opposition. This is often carried out by police or military.
- Authoritarian governments rely on indoctrination (instruction in the government's beliefs) to mold people's minds.
- Authoritarian governments spread propaganda. Control of all mass media (newspapers, TV, internet, etc.) allows this to happen.
- Authoritarian governments often create "enemies of the state" to blame for things that go wrong.

The presentation must also make specific comparisons to the novel *1984*.

Student Sample

The following images are slides from a group's presentation on Mohammed Bin Salman (MBS). These slides, in particular, focus on the murder of journalist Jamal Khashoggi, an example of an authoritarian leader's use of violence and manipulation of the media to maintain power. The slides juxtapose information about Khashoggi's murder with relevant quotations from *1984*.

It is worth noting that this student group conducted their research and prepared their presentation in December of 2018, when the story of Jamal Khashoggi was still developing. In some cases, these students were adding information that had been published that day.

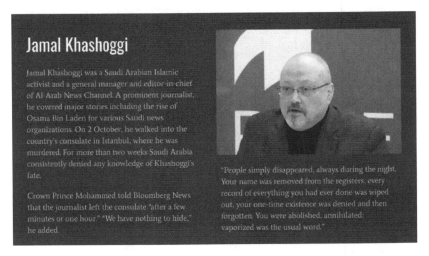

Figure 5.8   **Student Presentation on Authoritarianism in Today's World.**

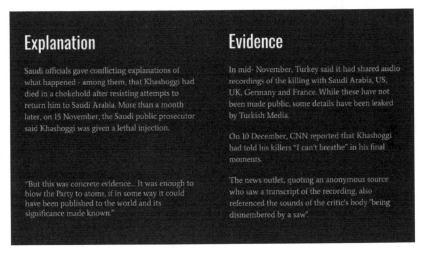

Figure 5.9   **Student Presentation on Authoritarianism in Today's World.**

1984 FINAL ESSAY

As a follow up to the research project, students will complete the unit by writing an essay on authoritarianism in contemporary society and in the novel *1984*. The essay must reference at least three authoritarian leaders; therefore, each student will write about two leaders that their group did not present on. It is important, then, that all students are taking copious notes as groups are presenting.

The essay should focus on the characteristics of authoritarian governments and authoritarian leaders (discussed in the research project). Finally, the essay must make specific comparisons to the novel *1984*.

CONCLUSION

Though Orwell's texts have been mainstays on syllabi for decades now, it seems the time has come to truly make them new and relevant again. We need students tuned into how language is used to corrupt and limit access to knowledge. We need students willing to speak up when power is asserting itself through the denial of objective truth. And we certainly need students who can recognize and be offended by the attempt to destroy or limit access to truth through technology, social media, or the repression or denial of the free press.

This unit allows students to face their own culpabilities with regard to blindly accepting the word of their "superiors" while also putting this lesson in the real-time context of authoritarian leaders from around the world. Students will be asked to recognize and address their own weaknesses and consider the potential ramifications of these same vulnerabilities. Truth is a hard thing to teach, but now more than ever, we need students tuned into how easily truth is manipulated and how essential it is to hold the line when we are told $2 + 2 = 5$.

NOTES

1. George Orwell, *Animal Farm* (London: Plume, 2003), 7.
2. Orwell, *Animal Farm*, 25.
3. George Orwell, *Nineteen Eighty-Four: A Novel* (New York, NY: Berkley, 2016), 14.
4. Orwell, *Nineteen Eighty-Four*, 11–15.
5. Orwell, *Animal Farm*, 59.
6. Ceylan Yeginsu, "Turkey Issues a Warrant for Fethullah Gulen, Cleric Accused in Coup," The New York Times (The New York Times, August 4, 2016), https://www.nytimes.com/2016/08/05/world/europe/turkey-erdogan-fethullah-gulen .html.
7. Orwell, *Nineteen Eighty-Four*, 46.
8. Orwell, *Nineteen Eighty-Four*, 47.
9. Orwell, *Nineteen Eighty-Four*, 51.
10. Orwell, *Nineteen Eighty-Four*, 52.
11. Orwell, *Nineteen Eighty-Four*, 80.
12. Orwell, *Nineteen Eighty-Four*, 81.

Chapter 6

Genocide and Ethnic Internment in *Night* and *Farewell to Manzanar*

Perhaps the most devastating and most extreme consequence of Otherness and dehumanization is genocide. In the ultimate real-life example of the potential dangers of Otherness, this chapter will explore the mass internment and mass extermination of groups of people.

In 2018, a study commissioned by the Conference on Jewish Material Claims against Germany found that 22 percent of millennials—also known as Generation Y—have never heard of the Holocaust.[1] This is a staggering statistic, and it should alert the larger community of educators to the need to teach our current generation of students—Generation Z—and all the generations to follow, the truth of the Holocaust.

The stakes for such teaching could not be higher, as its primary goal is to prevent something like the Holocaust from ever happening again. This chapter is being written in the midst of the 2020 Coronavirus pandemic, a time when harassment and violence against people of Asian descent have increased because of the virus's purported Chinese origins. The perpetrators of such harassment and violence have imposed blame for the virus on a perceived Other, and there is no better demonstration of the dangers of such thinking, or of its ability to spread like wildfire, than the Holocaust.

Therefore, the Holocaust must be taught early and often, and in our middle and high school English classrooms, an effective tool for such teaching is literature, such as Elie Wiesel's *Night* or *The Diary of Anne Frank*—firsthand accounts of a Holocaust survivor and of one its victims, respectively.

Furthermore, as teachers in the United States, we cannot—and must not—neglect to teach the uglier parts of our own history. While Japanese

Internment is certainly not an atrocity on the level of the Holocaust, it is certainly important for students to know that in the same year that Elie Wiesel was locked in a ghetto with all of his Jewish neighbors, the U.S. government ordered all Americans of Japanese descent to abandon their homes (and most of their belongings) and to be detained in designated camps, an experience described firsthand by Jeanne Wakatsuki Houston in the memoir *Farewell to Manzanar.*

This chapter not only will provide strategies for using literary memoirs such as *Night* and *Farewell to Manzanar* to teach historical events—the Holocaust and Japanese Internment, respectively—but will also model how to expand and connect students' new knowledge of those events to similar atrocities that are occurring in our world today.

READING *NIGHT*

Activity One: Contextual Research on the Holocaust

I have more faith in Hitler than in anyone else. He alone has kept his promises, all his promises, to the Jewish people.[2]

Because many students of middle or high school age bring little prior knowledge of the Holocaust to the table, a good place to begin is with some research.

Assign groups of students one (or, in smaller classes, one or two) of the following topics. Students should research the topic and prepare a presentation to deliver to the class. The goal of the presentation is to inform their audience, and it may be helpful, as they prepare, to imagine an audience that knows absolutely nothing about the topic. What is the essential information that such an audience should know?

- Adolf Hitler/The Nazi Party
- The German Invasion of Poland (1939)
- Jewish Ghettos during the Holocaust
- Auschwitz Concentration Camp
- Buna Concentration Camp
- Buchenwald Concentration Camp
- Anne Frank
- Nuremberg Trials
- Kristallnacht (Night of Broken Glass)
- Death Marches during the Holocaust
- Josef Mengele
- The Final Solution

Be sure to instruct students to include a Works Cited slide at the end of their presentation. You can also instruct them to include in-text citations (as either parentheticals or footnotes) for the information on each slide. This would also be an appropriate time to teach—or reinforce—strategies for evaluating the credibility of sources.

Activity Two: Comparing Family Separation

I didn't know that this was the moment in time and the place where I was leaving my mother and Tzipora forever.[3]

When students read of Elie Wiesel's separation from his mother and sister upon arrival at the Buchenwald camp, they may make a connection to the 2018 crisis in which waves of asylum seekers from Central America overwhelmed the U.S. immigration system. In an effort to reduce the influx, the United States enacted a policy in which the children of detained asylum seekers would be separated from their parents. In total, over 5,000 children were separated from their parents in 2018 and 2019.

Just as Elie Wiesel's account of his separation depicts the experience of thousands, the story of one child can help students understand the broader crisis of 2018. One such example is five-year-old Filomena, whose story was depicted in a comic strip by KQED News cartoonist Mark Fiore.[4]

The comic strip is adapted from a KQED News radio story by Tyche Hendricks titled, "One Migrant Family's Story of Separation at the Border."[5]

Have students read the comic strip and listen to the article. Then, instruct them to write a paragraph comparing/contrasting Filomena's experience of family separation with that of Elie Wiesel, as described in Chapter 2 of *Night*.

Activity Three: Theme of Dehumanization

In a few seconds, we had ceased to be men.[6]

As discussed in chapter 5, one of the consequences—and often one of the goals—of Otherness is the dehumanization of the other, and students should recognize that dehumanization is a central theme of *Night*.

Students should understand that dehumanization is the taking away of a person's (or a group of people's) humanity, or their human characteristics.

Through the group research presentations at the beginning of the unit, students should already be familiar with the extent of the Nazi party's efforts to dehumanize Jews, both through propaganda and policy.

As students read *Night*, they should collect quotations from the text that establish and help develop this theme.

Early examples in the novel include the Jews of Sighet being herded into cattle cars and later branded with numbers on their arm. These particular examples reflect a common method of dehumanization—the replacement of human behavior or treatment with animal behavior or treatment.

We also see the theme of dehumanization reflected in Elie's transformation throughout the novel. An early example of this comes when he fails to act—or even to feel anything—when his father is beaten. From this moment on, Elie finds it more and more difficult to recognize himself, a struggle that culminates in the memoir's final image, when Elie looks into a mirror and fails not only to recognize himself but also to see a living human being; rather, he sees a corpse.

The quotations that students collect could be used for a variety of assignments focused on the theme of dehumanization, such as a timed writing, formal essay, class discussion, or class presentation. Students can also use these quotations in the assignment on intertextuality between *Night* and *Farewell to Manzanar*, described below.

READING *FAREWELL TO MANZANAR*

As mentioned earlier, at the time that Elie Wiesel and his family were being forced from their home and moved to a concentration camp, the U.S. government was enacting a policy that required all American citizens of Japanese descent to leave their own homes and relocate to internment camps. Jeanne Wakatsuki Houston was one such citizen, and she describes her experience during internment in the memoir, *Farewell to Manzanar*, co-written with James D. Houston.

Farewell to Manzanar is a book that pairs well with Wiesel's *Night* and provides students further insight into the effects—and dangers—of policies rooted in Otherness.

Activity Four: Contextual Research on Japanese Internment

But at the time, it was pure chaos. That's the only way to describe it. The evacuation had been so hurriedly planned, the camps so hastily thrown together, nothing was completed when we got there, and almost nothing worked.[7]

As it was with the Holocaust, students will likely bring to class a varied but ultimately limited prior knowledge of Japanese Internment. Therefore, it is necessary that they do some research and present the findings of that research.

Assign students (or groups of students) one of the following topics, and instruct them to prepare a presentation to deliver to the class. Again, the purpose of the presentation is to inform an audience that, for the most part, has no knowledge whatsoever of the topic.

- Executive Order 9066
- Civilian Exclusion Order No. 34
- Pearl Harbor
- Manzanar War Relocation Center
- Manzanar Riot (December 1942)
- War Relocation Authority "Application for Leave Clearance"
- Jeanne Wakatsuki Houston

INTERTEXTUALITY BETWEEN *NIGHT* AND *FAREWELL TO MANZANAR*

As students read the memoir, *Farewell to Manzanar*, they should keep notes on similarities and differences between the experiences of Elie, in *Night*, and Jeanne, in *Farewell to Manzanar*. This should also be a regular topic of discussion in class as students make their way through the chapters. These notes and discussions will prepare them for the timed writing to follow and for the final essay that will end the unit.

Activity Five: Comparing/Contrasting *Night* and *Farewell to Manzanar*

You cannot deport 110,000 people unless you have stopped seeing individuals. Of course, for such a thing to happen, there has to be a kind of acquiescence on the part of the victims, some submerged belief that this treatment is deserved, or at least allowable.[8]

Assign students a timed (single class period), in-class essay. The essay should compare and/or contrast the experiences of Elie Wiesel and Jeanne Wakatsuki Houston, as described in their respective memoirs.

Specifically, the timed writing should focus on the theme of dehumanization in the two works—the means and methods by which the narrators, and the people around them, were dehumanized, as well as the reasons and consequences behind those methods. Through this lens, students should be encouraged to apply the following related concepts to their comparison of the two texts:

- Otherness
- Identity

- Tribalism
- Alienation

GENOCIDE AND INTERNMENT TODAY

Both Wiesel and Houston have declared that the purpose of their memoir was to ensure that history does not repeat itself. That we never forget. Nevertheless, genocide and ethnic cleansing and mass incarceration of ethnic groups have continued, repeatedly, in the decades since.

It is important, therefore, that students are aware not only of the atrocities of the past but also of the atrocities in the world in which they live. The unit will now turn to two such ongoing atrocities against the following groups in the following countries:

- Uighur Muslims in China
- Rohingya Muslims in Myanmar

Internment of Uighur Muslims

Many students may know nothing about Uighur Muslims, but nearly all students will know about the video-sharing app TikTok.

In November of 2019, seventeen-year-old Feroza Aziz recorded a TikTok video that seemed to be a tutorial for using an eyelash curler. However, several seconds into the video, she urges her audience to research what is happening to Uighur Muslims in China and to raise awareness of the issue.

The video is in response to the Chinese government's internment of over a million Uighur Muslims in Xinjiang province. In the video, Aziz compares this internment to the Holocaust, describing the internment camps as concentration camps.

Shortly after the video was posted (and went viral), TikTok, which is owned by a Chinese company, removed the video and blocked Aziz's account, a move that caught the attention of the national news media. TikTok initially denied removing the video, but after extensive coverage by multiple news outlets of the video and its censoring, TikTok apologized and restored both the video and Aziz's account.

Similarly, the Chinese government initially denied the existence of the internment camps, but, after extensive coverage, they shifted to describing the camps as "education centers."

Because of our students' familiarity with TikTok and apps like it, as well as their closeness in age to Aziz, this video and the news stories that followed it is an effective way to introduce students to the issue of the current internment of Uighur Muslims in China.

Activity Six: Incorporating an Informational Text on Uighur Muslims

We can never afford to forget what happened at Manzanar and the other wartime camps. Those events remind us that this lesson must be learned and learned and learned again.[9]

Assign students the following article—or another current article on Uighur Muslims in China (see "Note" below)—to read and annotate, focusing their annotations on main ideas, claims, and key terms.

The article describes the Chinese government's efforts to use propaganda in mainstream and social media to discredit criticism (and possible U.S. sanctions) for their detainment and mistreatment of Uighur Muslims.

- "Facing Criticism Over Muslim Camps, China Says: What's the Problem?" by Chris Buckley and Austin Ramzy, *The New York Times*, December 9, 2019.[10]

As they read and annotate, students should answer the following questions in their notebook:

- Who created this document (person and/or organization)?
- When was this document created?
- What is the purpose of this document (to inform/to persuade/to entertain/ etc.)?
- What is the main idea (or claim) of this document?
- Rewrite that claim in the form of a question.
- List three pieces of evidence from the document that help answer that question.

Note: Because the plights of both Uighur and Rohingya Muslims are ongoing stories, they offer a unique opportunity in the classroom to teach and discuss events in real-time, as they are unfolding. For example, the article above, from December 9, 2019, as well as the article on Rohingya Genocide below, from December 11, 2019, was used in a lesson with students *on the same day* that the articles were published.

By taking advantage of such opportunities, we will impress upon our students the timelessness and universality of the topics we are exploring.

Rohingya Genocide

The internment of Uighur Muslims in China is not the only human rights atrocity currently happening in our world. In December of 2019, Aung San Suu Kyi, a former recipient of the Nobel Peace Prize, stood before the United Nations International Court of Justice to defend the killing and exile of Rohingya Muslims in her home country of Myanmar.

Aung San Suu Kyi did not deny that thousands of Rohingya had been killed and/or raped, nor that villages had been burned and nearly a million had been driven into exile. Rather, the Burmese diplomat argued against the United Nation's use of the term "genocide," instead of describing the Rohingya as a terrorist group, a common strategy of today's oppressive governments (as we saw in chapter 5), and the actions against the Rohingya as government efforts to suppress terrorism.

Activity Seven: Incorporating an Informational Text on the Rohingya Genocide

To forget would be not only dangerous but offensive; to forget the dead would be akin to killing them a second time.[11]

As before, assign students a current article on the Rohingya Genocide, such as the following report from *The New York Times*, which, as mentioned, was used in a lesson with students on the same day as its publication.

- "Aung San Suu Kyi Defends Myanmar Against Rohingya Genocide Accusations" by Marlise Simons and Hannah Beech, *The New York Times*, December 11, 2019.[12]

Again, students should read and annotate the article, with a focus on the following questions:

- Who created this document (person and/or organization)?
- When was this document created?
- What is the purpose of this document (to inform/to persuade/to entertain/etc.)?
- What is the main idea (or claim) of this document?
- Rewrite that claim in the form of a question.
- List three pieces of evidence from the document that help answer that question.

FINAL ASSESSMENTS

The following summative assignments will require students not only to conduct research of crimes against Uighurs and Rohingya but also to draw connections between those events and the events of the Holocaust and Japanese Internment, as described in *Night* and *Farewell to Manzanar*, respectively.

Both of the following—one group assignment and one individual assignment—will use the GRASPS model for meaningful assessment, developed by Grant Wiggins and Jay McTighe, authors of *Understanding by Design.*[13]

Genocide Awareness Campaign

The following group assignment will challenge students to conduct research for a specific purpose: to raise awareness in their school community of what is happening in China and Myanmar.

Because the issues in question are happening today, as we write this and as you read it, students have a unique opportunity to engage in a learning experience that is not a simulation. They will actually raise awareness on their campus and in their communities of these atrocities.

Genocide and Ethnic Cleansing Group Awareness Campaign

Goal: Your goal is to raise awareness of genocide and ethnic cleansing in China or Myanmar (your group will be assigned one or the other).

Role: You are a member of a committee whose job it is to inform our school community about the atrocities against Uighur Muslims in China or Rohingya Muslims in Myanmar.

Audience: The students, staff, and parents of our school

Situation: Despite the lessons of the Holocaust and Japanese Internment, large groups of people are still being murdered and/or imprisoned in the world today.

Product:

1. *Create a poster that will help raise awareness of the atrocities against Uighur Muslims in China or Rohingya Muslims in Myanmar (depending on which topic your group was assigned).*

2. *Prepare a five- to ten-minute presentation (to be given outside of our classroom) that will help raise awareness of these atrocities (using your poster as a visual aid).*

Success: Your poster and presentation will be graded using the following list of requirements:

- *A clear heading/title*
- *At least five facts from your research (with citations)*
- *At least two relevant quotations from the memoirs we read (one from Night and one from Farewell to Manzanar)*
- *At least one image (drawn or printed) that is appropriate for the Goal and Audience above*
- *A "call to action" (what could/should people do to help this situation)*

Once students have prepared their awareness campaign, help them to schedule presentations in various classrooms, in staff or department meetings, and in parent meetings. Repeated practice and delivery of their campaign will help them achieve the goal of raising awareness while simultaneously helping them achieve speaking and listening standards.

Student Samples

Figures 6.1, 6.2, 6.3, and 6.4 display examples of posters created by eighth grade students for the above assignment. Each team presented these posters in multiple venues—classrooms, faculty department meetings, and so on. The posters were then hung around the campus for several months.

Following the Story

Because the Uighur and Rohingya stories are ongoing, significant new developments continuously take place, even after the unit is over. As these developments occur, it is important to address them. To ignore them would suggest they were only "useful" to the classroom when we were directly studying them, and that is the exact wrong message to send. Consider embedding a procedure in your classroom that allows for "further consideration" of such events as they unfold. Perhaps students could report to the class on such developments, or they could post to a class-wide Google classroom discussion board.

Final Essay

After the awareness campaign is complete, assign students the following essay, which mirrors the group awareness campaign but is to be completed individually.

- *Goal: Your goal is to raise awareness of genocide and ethnic cleansing in China and Myanmar.*
- *Role: You are a member of a committee whose job it is to inform the school community about the atrocities against Uighur Muslims in China and Rohingya Muslims in Myanmar.*

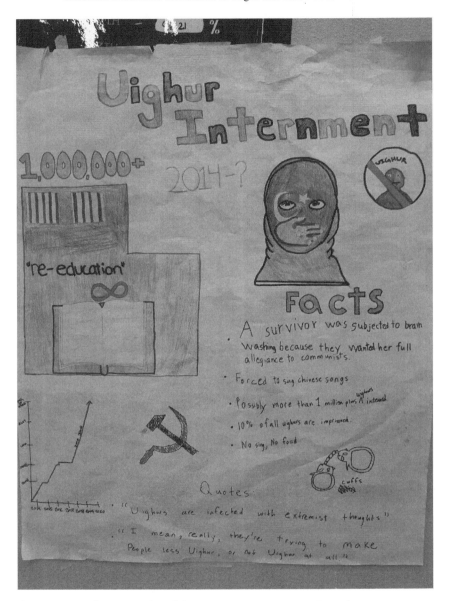

Figure 6.1   Student Poster for Uighur Internment Awareness Campaign.

- *Audience: Students, staff, and parents*
- *Situation: Despite the lessons of the Holocaust and Japanese Internment, large groups of people are still being murdered and/or imprisoned in the world today.*

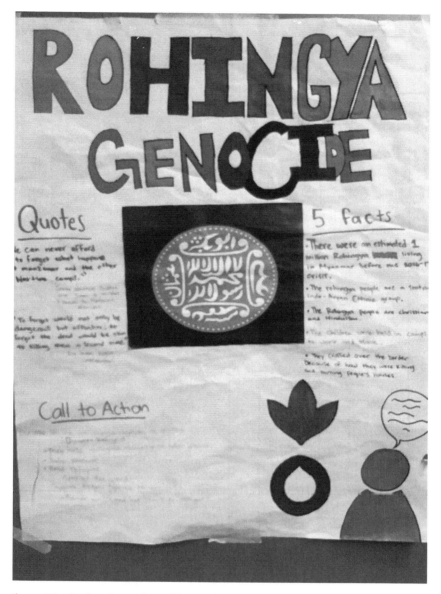

Figure 6.2   Student Poster for Rohingya Genocide Awareness Campaign.

- *Product: Write an essay (with an introduction, body, and conclusion) that compares the genocide and ethnic cleansing of Uighurs and Rohingya to the Holocaust and Japanese Internment, as described in Night and Farewell to Manzanar.*
- *Success: Your essay will be evaluated using the following guidelines and checklist:*

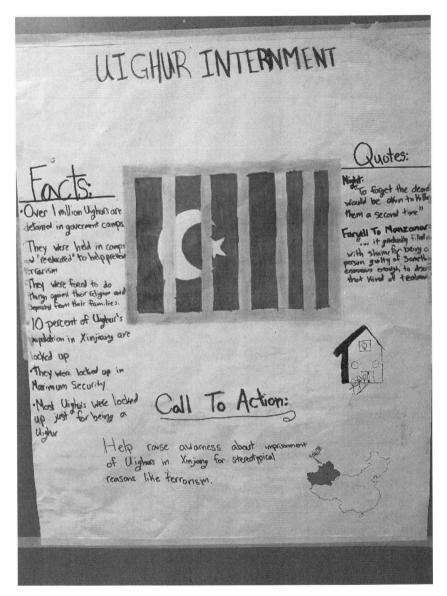

Figure 6.3   Student Poster for Uighur Internment Awareness Campaign.

Essay Guidelines

Introductory paragraph (three to five sentences—get in and get out)
- *Introduces topic*
- *Sets up the thesis*
- *Declares the thesis (what the essay will show or argue)*

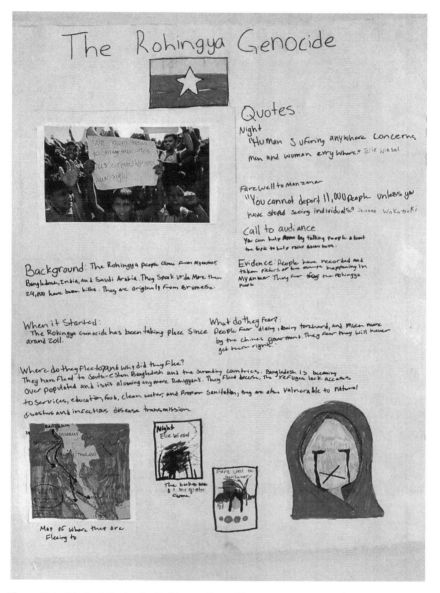

Figure 6.4   Student Poster for Rohingya Genocide Awareness Campaign.

Two or more body paragraphs (eight to eleven sentences each)
- *Topic sentence that makes a claim and supports the thesis*
- *Two to three specific examples + commentary (what it shows and why it is important)*

- *Transitional words and phrases that create a logical flow from one idea to the next*
- *Concluding sentence that reinforces the topic sentence/thesis and transitions to the next paragraph.*

Concluding paragraph (two to five sentences—get in and get out)
- *Restate thesis in a new, fresh way*
- *Summarize arguments presented in body paragraphs*
- *Finish with a final, definitive, bold statement*

Student Sample

The following is a sample response to the above prompt, written by an eigth grade student.

The memoirs Farewell to Manzanar *by Jeanne Wakatsuki, and* Night *by Elie Weasel, are true, firsthand accounts by survivors of horrible times in the mid-1900s. Japanese Internment and the Jewish Holocaust are well-known events that occurred in history, but many people are unaware of the horrors that are happening today. The Rohingya Genocide is happening in Myanmar, and the Uighur Internment is happening across China right now. You would think that we would recognize that these historical events that happened over fifty years ago are repeating themselves. I hope, as a member of the school committee, to inform the community and raise awareness about Uighur Muslim Interment and Rohingya Genocide.*

The Holocaust was a horrific event that occurred in the mid-nineteenth century. Jewish people were living throughout Europe when they were targeted due to their race. The Jewish were forced from their homes by Nazis, separated from their families, and placed in concentration camps, and more than six million Jews had been killed by the end of the Holocaust. The tragic event all started because Adolph Hitler believed that the Jews were beneath him. He believed that the Jews had no value as human beings, and his race was superior. After the Holocaust, it seemed like the idea of ethnic superiority was unheard of.

Until today, in Myanmar, where thousands of Rohingya Muslims are being persecuted for their ethnicity. The Rohingya Muslims are one of the largest ethnic groups in Myanmar. There were about one million Rohingya Muslims in Myanmar in 2017. However, Myanmar does not accept the Rohingya as a religion, nor citizens of Myanmar. Because of recent acts violence by the military, many Rohingya are fleeing Myanmar to other countries. Reports of military riots, burning villages, mass killings, and many women being raped by the Myanmar Military. As many as 781,000 were living in refugee camps in 2018.

Today, many people do not realize that the Rohingya Genocide is not very different from the Jewish Holocaust. Even though the Holocaust happened nearly eighty years ago, the Rohingya Genocide is very similar. For instance, during the Holocaust the Jews were forced out of their homes and into camps, but the Rohingya's villages are destroyed, and many are murdered. Thousands of Rohingya have been killed since 2017 while from 1941 to 1945; more than six million Jews were killed. Both the Rohingya and Jews were targeted because of their ethnicity. The Jewish Holocaust was an event where Jews were targeted and killed in mass numbers because of their religion. If we do not stop Rohingya Genocide, it will turn into another Holocaust. More people should be aware of these events, so we can prevent them in the future.

Rohingya Genocide is not the only issue occurring in the world today; the Uighur Muslims in China are being discriminated and held in prison-like camps, similar to the Japanese Internment. The Japanese Internment was a time where Japanese-Americans in the United States were removed from their homes because of their possible involvement in war operations and put into internment camps with little space, clothing, or access to the outside world. They were treated like enemies even though some had been U.S. citizens for many years. The Japanese were first imprisoned in 1942 when the evacuation order was first enforced; until 1946, when President Roosevelt rescinded the evacuation order. After the Japanese were released, many were unable to return to their previous homes, and it was difficult to find work. However, the U.S. government provided some aid to Japanese to help get their life back.

Similarly, Uighurs were first targeted in 2016 when the Chinese government started to recognize them as extremists. China is a mostly Buddhist country, and they saw the Uighur people as a threat to their religious status. At the start, China's government denied that these camps existed, then some documents leaked, and China now claims they are only running "reeducation facilities" for vocational trainees. Released detainees claim that they were held in a prison-like environment, where they are taught Mandarin, learn Chinese hymns, and write "self-criticism essays"; these are all things that are meant to encourage Uighur Muslims to abandon their faith. There are about 500 "reeducation centers" across China that are surrounded by barbed-wire fences and guards who do not allow visitors. Additionally, any reporters that visited the inside of these facilities were always escorted by government officials. Many Uighurs are placed in these centers because of illegal religious videos, praying at Muslim funerals, or even wearing a burqa. Individuals that have been released, claim that they are basically brainwashed in classrooms all day, and they are given little food. Many women also reported being raped. I would say that we should take action to prevent another internment, but it seems as though it's already happening, and we need to stop it before more Uighurs are affected.

The Japanese Internment that happened in the nineteen-forties, and the Uighur Internment that is currently happening in China, have many similarities. In both cases, a specific group of people was targeted because of their ethnicity and imprisoned by the government. The Japanese-Americans were held because the U.S. military was worried that these citizens would try to betray the U.S. during the war. The Uighurs are being captured and held in facilities because the Chinese government is hoping to "cleanse" China's population of Uighurs, or at least try to teach the Uighurs Chinese practice. While all of the Japanese were released at the end of the interment, many Uighurs remain in the camps until they are allowed to return to the outside world, and this could take weeks, months, or even years. Both the Japanese and the Uighurs were/are held in extreme conditions during their internment.

To review, Rohingya Genocide in Myanmar and Uighur internment in China are huge issues occurring in our world today. Rohingya Muslims are being killed in mass quantities in Myanmar, and Uighur Muslims are being held in "reeducation" facilities, where they are forced to learn Chinese culture in a prison-like environment. These events are very similar to past events such as the Jewish Holocaust and the Japanese Interment. We should be learning from our past mistakes, but instead we are letting history repeat itself. It is very frightening to know that these issues are happening right in front of us, but nothing is being done about it. I hope my essay has informed you about the current issues of our world and raised awareness about them. I hope as a member of the Franklin High School Committee, that I have done my duty of informing the world about serious issues.

CONCLUSION

This chapter has demonstrated how to incorporate seminal works of literature into your curriculum while making "old" texts of "resolved" problems absolutely representative of current daily life. Teaching something like *Night* reverently isn't enough. Using it as an example of memoir or to use it in conjunction with your World War II unit isn't enough. A memoir looks back. A history unit looks back. *Night* is happening today, right now, to people around the world.

By examining two texts that show the extreme of what perceived Otherness can do to entire groups of people, students will come to recognize patterns that are still manifesting around the world and that still demand us to bear witness and get involved. This is a chapter in which teachers should particularly feel empowered to reimagine what is presented here to fit whatever the new day brings. We need students watching the world around them, educating themselves about what is going on, and engaging in educating others. And, if we at all can, we need to provide them the tools necessary to investigate the world around them, to sound the alarm when necessary, and to prove to them that they (just like that young girl and her TikTok video) have all they need to get the world to listen.

We cannot read *Night* and then move on—*Night* is a call to action, a demand that we bear witness to what has happened in the past and that we refuse to tolerate it happening again.

NOTES

1. "New Survey by Claims Conference Finds Significant Lack of Holocaust Knowledge in the United States," Claims Conference, accessed July 17, 2020, http://www.claimscon.org/study/.

2. Elie Wiesel, *Night*, trans. Marion Wiesel (New York, NY: Hill and Wang, 2006), 81.

3. Wiesel, *Night*, 29.

4. Mark Fiore, "One Family's Story of Separation: A Cartoon Account," KQED, accessed June 26, 2018, https://www.kqed.org/news/11677170/one-familys-story-of-separation-a-cartoon-account.

5. Tyche Hendricks, "One Migrant Family's Story of Separation at the Border," KQED, accessed June 26, 2018, https://www.kqed.org/news/11677196/one-migrant-familys-story-of-separation-at-the-border.

6. Wiesel, *Night*, 37.

7. Jeanne Wakatsuki Houston and James D. Houston, *Farewell to Manzanar* (Boston, MA: Houghton Mifflin, 2017), 27.

8. Wakatsuki Houston, *Farewell to Manzanar*, 142.

9. Wakatsuki Houston, *Farewell to Manzanar*, 188.

10. Chris Buckley and Austin Ramzy, "Facing Criticism Over Muslim Camps, China Says: What's the Problem?" The New York Times (The New York Times, December 9, 2019), https://www.nytimes.com/2019/12/09/world/asia/china-camps-muslims.html.

11. Wiesel, *Night*, xv.

12. Marlise Simons and Hannah Beech, "Aung San Suu Kyi Defends Myanmar Against Rohingya Genocide Accusations," The New York Times (The New York Times, December 11, 2019), https://www.nytimes.com/2019/12/11/world/asia/aung-san-suu-kyi-rohingya-myanmar-genocide-hague.html.

13. Grant P. Wiggins and Jay McTighe, *Understanding by Design* (Alexandria, VA: Association for Supervision and Curriculum Development, 2008).

Chapter 7

Gender Inequality and
the Handmaid's Tale

The world can often seem overwhelming with its incessant sea of troubles. It's hard to pick problems to work on because there are just so many from which to choose. Injustice is all around us, and making headway on problems is slow and aggravating work.

For this reason, trying to convince people that something so seemingly benign like word choice is one of those problems can be a tough sell. But it's true. How we talk about issues and about each other frames narratives. Words used (or unused) create emotional, visceral responses. Language can seem abstract and beside the point in the face of injustice, but when we lose control over language, we lose control of the problem.

How we talk (and have always talked) about women is consistently illuminating and troubling. The words applied to questions of gender are often purposeful and loaded, and despite our varying opinions on these issues, we must acknowledge that language has been a tool of conversion for both sides of the aisle.

So far in this book, we have considered racial injustice, religious bias, and the ripple effect of abusive policy practices—all of which is utterly important and should be meaningfully tied into our curriculum as often as possible.

No matter what your student population is, and no matter what type of community you live in, half of your students are probably female. As such, it is of the utmost importance to include time within your syllabus to really reach out and examine the question of gender and sexism in society.

For generations (and continuing into today) most students will read a narrow set of texts in their English Language Arts classes that is mostly a reflection of the white male experience. It is important to create a syllabus that celebrates and acknowledges diversity. That means any reading list should aim to be composed of at least 50% female authors and/or feature more female protagonists.

Students (male and female) need stories that explore the female experience, and Scout Finch's idyllic childhood just isn't enough. This may be potentially divisive. Do it anyway. We need a generation of students who can talk to each other and make headway, particularly on topics such as the Equal Rights Amendment, the wage gap, sexual assault, and abortion.

There are very few issues that Americans feel more strongly about than the question of abortion, so the first thing you need to get your students to hear you say is: This is not going to be a pro-choice unit or a pro-life unit. This unit will not have a political agenda. This unit will strive to turn down the noise and immediate, visceral, knee-jerk reactions, and get us each to a place where we can understand both sides of an argument about which we may feel very strongly.

Though this will not be a unit on the question of abortion, it will certainly be a unit on how societies legislate, police, and equivocate about women's bodies, with or without a pregnancy involved. That is the anchor of this unit: what does it mean, and what may be at risk, if you are a woman? To what extent is your body your own, and to what extent can what happens to your body be dictated merely by your sex?

Additionally, this text allows an opportunity to reimagine questions of identity and personhood through a distinctly female lens. What does it mean to be female in society? In the past and in the present? What is more important, what a body *can* do, or what you *want* your own body to do?

It is important to note that Atwood doesn't consider *The Handmaid's Tale* strictly dystopian, and certainly not in the Science Fiction genre. Rather, she suggests this text is something else: "speculative fiction." As she has said in several interviews, everything in this text has happened at some point to some group throughout history. And it is this historical precedent that demands we have uncomfortable conversations about where we have been and where, perhaps, we still are in some areas (and where we may be going). Only then can forward momentum occur.

ACTIVITY ONE: REIMAGINE YOUR CLASSROOM SPACE

Truly amazing, what people can get used to, as long as there are a few compensations.[1]

What follows is a case study in what happens to a classroom dynamic if the teacher begins demonstrating prejudice against a gender.

This year my classroom looked a little different than normal. I have tables, not desks, and I arranged them in groups. Each table group was labeled with the setting from one of our novels that year (Oceania, West Egg, Elsinore, etc.) Gilead had always been present as a table group.

On the first day of the *Handmaid's* unit, I rearranged my tables into straight rows, with everyone facing forward. And on *every* table, I wrote a card labeling that space "Gilead." Of course the students noticed right away. Mostly, they were preoccupied with who they were sitting near. But the intention was clear; in this text, setting is everything. When you lose the ability to know about things beyond your immediate circumstances, you lose the ability to demand a better life. Normal is normal, even if normal is terrible. As Atwood writes, "Ordinary, said Aunt Lydia, is what you are used to. This may not seem ordinary to you now, but after a time it will. It will become ordinary."[2]

This is one of the great tasks Atwood accomplishes—she personifies how the simple lack of choice in one's life can quickly devolve into a lack of an identity, a lack of a real life.

The next step was to change the language used when greeting students into the classroom space for the day. I asked the "gentlemen" students to please sit on the left hand of the class, and the "girls" to sit on the right. Much to my surprise, they obeyed—and I use that word, "obey," consciously.

I then gave a reading quiz about the first few chapters of the novel. I handed out the gentlemen's quizzes first, and I also let them start as soon as they had a paper. Then I handed out the same quiz to the girls. They had less time to accomplish the task. One student sighed, but that was it. They continued to *obey*.

When time was up, I let the gentlemen correct their own quizzes, but the girls had to switch papers. We graded them all as a group (our normal procedure), but this time I only called on the boys for the answers. I totally ignored the girls' raised hands. I was overly solicitous to the boys, thanking them for each answer, and if it was wrong, helping them to the right one. I even told the boys to write in the correct answer, while insisting it was still "pencils down" for the girls' side of the room.

Still, in a room where I have a great rapport with students, no one said a thing.

Finally, I told the "gentlemen" that the quiz was worth ten points for them but worth one hundred for the girls. At this point, the girls were clearly annoyed. A boy raised his hand and asked what was going on, why was I treating the girls differently? I told him it was good for gentlemen to ask questions about their surroundings, but to not bother his head about this. I was handling it, I promised. And the questioning stopped. That was it. One sad, easily-squashed question.

Finally, I broke. I couldn't take the girls' quiet seething. Actually, the seething was understandable. It was the *silence* of their anger that worried me most. When I finally discontinued the charade and asked what they had noticed, the girls in the class made the following observations:

1. I called them "girls," but the boys were "gentlemen," which was more respectful, and drew attention to the dismissive, belittling diction of "girls," particularly when it wasn't matched by "boys" on the other side of the room.
2. The boys got more time to prove their knowledge on the test ("even though they probably didn't study like we did" a female student grumbled).
3. The boys didn't have their grades as adversely affected by the quiz as the girls did; they were disproportionately punished, merely for being girls.
4. I denied them the chance to participate. I acted like I didn't see them there, as if I had all the information I needed from the left side of the room and what the boys were saying.

They are smart cookies, and they understood the connections to the book without much hand-holding. When finally allowed to speak, they were more than a little peeved. When given permission to speak again, they wanted me to know how crummy it had felt. But when I said, "why did you let me get away with it?" they didn't have much to say. "Because you're the teacher!" one female student shouted, clearly aggravated with me. My response was, if I am clearly being unjust, does that still matter?

What we had uncovered was that the female student population knew they were being mistreated, but they only expressed their anger and resentment when they were *given permission* to be angry. Only when they knew it wouldn't be impolite—a worrisome occurrence that I hope isn't repeated in your own classrooms, if you choose to try this experiment.

The boy who had politely asked what was going on said, "But I did say something!" The reply was, "You said one thing and didn't push for change. And now you want to be congratulated for sorta kinda saying something when you clearly had been granted more power in the classroom than the girls. When you sensed I didn't like your question you backed down. What does that say about your character? Your willingness to go along?"

And to the rest of the boys in the room: Look how you let it happen. Look how you saw that you were at an advantage and you let someone be mistreated, dehumanized. Look how you took what you hadn't earned without a thought. Look how you let language change, and opportunities change, because you benefited from the change.

One male student said, "If they didn't like it, they could have done something."

Another male student said, "Well, it wasn't happening to me."

Another male student said, "I feel terrible."

Exactly.

I can think of no better way to begin a novel about the cost/benefit analysis of taking a stand when you know something in society is wrong. A major takeaway from the text is how easy it is to know something is wrong, and how hard it is to galvanize an individual, much less a society, to fight against those wrongs. And yet, what other choice do societies have?

Consider keeping your class separated by gender for the remainder of the unit. Studying a text with students who have previously co-mingled and are now forced into separation—like Offred's world in *The Handmaid's Tale*—and then mirroring that same gender-segregation in the classroom, will continue to provide revelations throughout the unit. For instance, the female students leaned on each other and seemed to absolutely absorb the lesson from the text that a team effort was the way forward. The male students, for their part, mentioned again and again how they had...

- ...never heard of these issues
- ...never thought of these issues
- ...never been taught these issues

It was remarkable, in real-time, to witness young men coming to grips with the fact that there were issues of civil rights that they were totally unaware of all around them, affecting people they knew and loved.

ACTIVITY TWO: WHAT DO YOU WANT FOR YOU, AND WHAT DO YOU WANT FOR YOUR SOCIETY?

That was when they suspended the Constitution. They said it would be temporary. There wasn't even any rioting in the streets. People stayed home at night, watching television, looking for some direction. There wasn't even an enemy you could put your finger on.[3]

One lesson Atwood teaches her audience in this text is to pay attention to the difference between what people want for their society and what they want for themselves. It makes a certain logical sense—a group needs group rules, and individuals can be granted more space, theoretically.

Consider the following activity as a way to have students reflect on what they value for themselves versus what they value in a society.

Put the following list on the board:

 1. Equality
 2. Human existence continuing
 3. Autonomy
 4. Religion
 5. Government
 6. Personal relationships
 7. Parenting
 8. Personhood
 9. Obedience
10. Family Values

Have students first rank their priorities from the above list for themselves. What do they value the most and what do they value the least in their own lives?

In the past, students have, for the most part, put major emphasis on (have you guessed?)

• Personal relationships
• Family values
• Autonomy

Then do the ranking again, but change the question to "What do you value the most in the society in which you live?" It has been fascinating to see the differences between the two lists.

The second list reflects how we want others to behave. For instance, people want a degree of obedience in society. We want people to stop at red lights and pay their taxes. And yet, far fewer of us worry about the value of obeying when it comes to our own behavior. When it is about *us*, autonomy often outranks obedience. But why?

Have students do a five minute written reflection on what their lists revealed about themselves. Did it suggest a selfishness? A yearning for personal freedom above others? Did it show an unwillingness to challenge authority? Do our priorities for societies change, and why?

How do our lists reflect the text, itself? To what degree does Atwood hold Offred accountable for her passivity prior to and during Gilead's ascension? And at the same time, how is this character defect so humanizing? How does this choice serve as a mirror for our own culpability?

This is a useful way to enter into Margaret Atwood's *The Handmaid's Tale*. What we want for ourselves rarely matches what we want from society. Offred, our protagonist, often remembers her life before the rise of Gilead. So many of these reminiscences focus on moments where something clearly unjust was going on, but she failed to grasp the severity of it, and rather passively accepted it. For instance,

*The newspaper stories were like dreams to us, bad dreams dreamt by others.
How awful, we would say, and they were, but they were awful without being
believable. They were too melodramatic, they had a dimension that was not
the dimension of our lives. We were the people who were not in the papers. We
lived in the blank white spaces at the edges of print. It gave us more freedom.
We lived in the gaps between the stories.*[4]

Part of the idea of society is doing what is right for the greater good. When
we can think only of ourselves, our wants, our desires—when, in short, we
are starring in our own movie, we can be more hedonistic. The above quote
demonstrates Offred knew society was struggling, and it was vaguely terrible. But the terror wasn't her life, so she didn't care overly much. She was
unable to imagine that what was happening abstractly in society could possibly land squarely on her doorstep. So, the novel asks, why do we assume
the individual life is more important than the life of the whole? And if it is,
how sustainable is society anyway?

ACTIVITY THREE: QUICKWRITE ON FEMINISM

We are a society dying, said Aunt Lydia, of too much choice.[5]

When students come in the room for the day, immediately have them write
for five or so minutes on the following prompt: What does the word *feminism*
mean to you? And what connotations of the word are you familiar with?

Let students write about both their own understanding of the word as well
as the connotations the word brings with it. Facilitate a discussion about what
they wrote. How did they get their connotative understanding? Was it another
example of tribalism and inherited perceptions? Did they see a connotation of
the word in the media somewhere?

The definition of feminism, according to the Oxford Dictionary, is this: the
advocacy of women's rights on the basis of the equality of the sexes.[6] That's
it. It doesn't declare only women can be feminists, and there is nothing anti-
male about feminism. It is the "radical notion" that women are deserving of
the same rights as men.

So why has society appropriated the word and made it dangerous?
Aggressive? Negative? And how does that appropriation foreshadow additional problems in the text?

You may not have time to discuss the rise of the feminist movement along-
side the rise of the Civil Rights movement in the 1960s and '70s, and that is
okay. But it is worth noting that this is the era in which Offred's mother was
a young woman, an era of militant activism to change society and provide
more equal lives for women.

Offred's mother is no hero in the text, but she is an important bridge to understanding a very simple idea: it is hard to appreciate that which you have always had. It is much easier to appreciate something if you had to fight tooth and nail to get it.

Offred (or whoever she was before she was Offred) did not need to fight for women's rights—she inherited them. And because of this, she never appreciates (until it is far too late) just how precarious her rights are as a woman. That which can be given can also be taken away.

For real-life applicability, consider having students study the rise and fall of the Equal Rights Amendment. This piece of legislation was thought to be a sure-fire, obvious win when it was introduced in the legislature. But now, fifty years later, it still is not part of the law.

ACTIVITY FOUR: DO WE EVEN NEED AN EQUAL RIGHTS AMENDMENT?

You are a transitional generation, said Aunt Lydia. It is the hardest for you. We know the sacrifices you are being expected to make. It is hard when men revile you. For the ones who come after you, it will be easier. They will accept their duties with willing hearts.

She did not say: Because they will have no memories of any other way.

She said: Because they won't want things they can't have.[7]

Nationally, we continue to debate how much legislation is necessary to conduct our society. Perhaps one of the longest legislative fights that has ebbed and flowed throughout the last few generations is the question of the Equal Rights Amendment.

Consider having students research the ERA to see how it has become another example of a logjam. Why can't people get behind it? What are the arguments for it? Against it? What can we infer about a society who A) claims to need such a law and B) cannot agree to pass such a law?

Sometimes students are shocked by the statistics seen below. That's understandable—this list of now-inherited rights seems totally natural to us and our society. But the teachable moment here really needs to be that it is hard to maintain an appreciation for a right you inherited. If you didn't have to fight for it, it might seem totally normal that you have it. And that complacency may result in losing or stagnating further progress toward equality.

This idea is personified between Offred and her real mother. Her mother, a radical feminist, is extreme in her views, and embarrassing when she visits. But part of that embarrassment is that she had to fight for women's equality so that her child could inherit a fairer world. The unintended consequence is the passivity of Offred and her generation. They didn't have to fight for equality, they were raised with it. And as such, equality became a far less valuable asset that they didn't know they were losing until it was lost.

Things Women Couldn't Do in the 1960s

The following list is based on Katie McLaughlin's 2014 CNN report, "5 Things Women Couldn't Do in the 1960s":[8]

1. Women could not get a credit card if they were unmarried. If they *were* married, the husband would need to co-sign. This did not apply to single men. (This remained the case until 1974).
2. Serve on a jury of their "peers." It wasn't until 1973 that women could serve on juries in all fifty states.
3. Use birth control when they wanted. Though created in the 1950s it was only for "health reasons" and could *only* be prescribed to married women, and was *rarely* stocked by pharmacies. That remained the case for a *generation*—into the 1970s.
4. Get an Ivy League Education. Women were finally admitted to Yale in 1969. Harvard in 1977. Columbia in 1981.
5. Equality in the workforce. In 1963, women made $0.59 for every dollar men made doing the same work. Today, women make $0.82 for every dollar men make, and Hispanic women make only $0.58.

So not yet!

These statistics can be really bothersome to students, and understandably so. The following information demonstrates a bit more of a submerged sexism that still affects women in the workplace, and a workplace all of your students will be familiar with.

Consider the following statistics, based on Denise R. Superville's 2016 article, "Few Women Run the Nation's School Districts. Why?" in *Education Week*:[9]

- Women make up over 75% of the teaching industry. Teachers make, on average, $60,000 a year.
- Slightly more than 50% of principals are women. Principals, on average, make $75,000.
- Women make up fewer than 25% of school superintendents, who make, on average, $180,000.

Now, how on Earth can a profession that is in every city, every town in America be overwhelmingly staffed by women, and yet, the higher up the ladder one climbs, the less opportunity there is? For a profession that has been traditionally (and is still currently) overwhelmingly female?

This may be an opportunity for some outside research. Teaching and school districts is something familiar to our students. But what about jobs that they may have dreams about? What about the CEOs? How many women are running major companies? And what are their salaries as compared to their male counterparts?

Let your students make inferences about the data, and give them time to discuss these inferences in class. The numbers tell their own story. See what they come up with.

A common inference about the teaching profession is that those higher up in school districts are unwilling to work for a woman, or be led by a woman. Even though it is a profession of overwhelming female participation, women are not often allowed to run the systems that affect them most directly.

It is at this point in the unit students start telling their stories of being called "too bossy" at ages 5 or 4 or 3 years old. Female students might tell you about being gifted and constantly paired with the lowest-achieving students in their classes so that they can be "a model" for them, whereas their gifted male counterparts are never expected to do the same thing for their peers.

Girls are still taught, implicitly or explicitly, if they are to lead, they must do so gently. They must not be seen to be pushy. They are not to be angry. They are not to be exasperated. They are to model good behavior. When they are little, the word applied to such behavior is *bossy*. When they are adults applying for jobs that pay more, where they will be supervising men, the word often turns to another B-word. And still, we work in a society that values "leadership" qualities in men but is unwilling to work for a "bitchy" boss.

After considering these data, and perhaps any other information they can find, do the sexes seem equal in society? Are economic opportunities equal? Are opportunities for independence equal? If not, what more work is there to be done?

ACTIVITY FIVE: INTERTEXTUALITY IN THE EPIGRAPH

The Handmaid's Tale begins with a trio of epigraphs, each independently important to the text, and each a major component to an in-tandem understanding. They are as follows:

And when Rachel saw that she bore Jacob no children, Rachel envied her sister, and said unto Jacob, Give me children or else I die.

And Jacob's anger was kindled against Rachel, and he said, Am I in God's stead, who hath withheld from thee the fruit of the womb?

And she said, Behold my maid Bilhah, go in unto her, and she shall bear upon my knees, that I may also have children by her.

—*Genesis 30: 1-3*

But as to myself, having been wearied out for many years with offering vain, idle, visionary thoughts, and at length utterly despairing of success, I fortunately fell upon this proposal...

—*Jonathan Swift,* A Modest Proposal

In the desert there is no sign that says, Thou shalt not eat stones.

—*Sufi Proverb*[10]

Have students work in small groups and devise a thesis statement about their interpretation of the intertextuality between these disparate beginnings. Let them google a bit, research the context of each if they are unfamiliar, and then have them declare (maybe have them put it on a whiteboard for the class) what connections they see.

This activity can demonstrate a few things: how many works and events led to Atwood's "speculative fiction" and how an interplay of multiple points of view is going to be really powerful. My favorite student-generated thesis was simply this: "don't assume we won't try our worst ideas." Perfect, right?

Additionally, this activity introduces the idea that the book deals with questions of appropriating language and manipulating it for one's own selfish goals. Just as in *The Merchant of Venice,* we have a power structure here that maintains power based on what the powerful get to say about the powerless, and how the powerful frame the narrative. The oft-repeated verses from the Book of Genesis are taken and repeated as an *excerpt* of a larger body of text, and yet are never represented as such.

Why, though, does Atwood begin like this? And why the seeming inability to pick a lane, and choose one quote? How does each contribute to the text, and how do they bleed together?

ACTIVITY SIX: FREEDOM TO AND FREEDOM FROM

You used to have freedom to. Now you have freedom from. Don't underrate it.[11]

Gilead has gained power by what it claims to be able to give to society. It can increase a flat-lined birth rate. It can prevent crime. It can clean up the environment. Gileadeans will be free from a lot of existential threats. But they have surrendered their freedom to...choose partners, choose love, control their bodies, control their money, control their names, and on and on.

In the face of mass crises, all of which could adversely affect human existence as we know it, what should take precedence: personal freedom, or a society free from a number of problems?

As this is being written, we are in the throes of the Coronavirus pandemic, and people around the country have begun politicizing the wearing of a mask in public spaces. Groups of people are storming capital buildings with guns, demanding to end the lockdown. People are blocking the streets that lead to hospitals. They are demanding their "freedoms." There have been countless other examples such as this—demonstrations demanding personal freedom—within the past century.

Have students choose a moment of civil unrest when personal freedom was pitted against societal values. For instance, the 2017 Women's March was the largest march in United States history. Its aim was to demand autonomy over women's own bodies. In this way, the protests against the COVID-19 lockdown and the women's march have something in common: they both are aimed at having individual control over one's body.

But this demonstrates something that any society will have to wrestle with: there is sometimes ambiguity between what we want for ourselves and our bodies, and what is "good" for society. This discomfort between two sides is often how growth happens. But does it necessarily follow that the individual's wants are always superior to society's desires?

Gilead rose to power (as so many totalitarian regimes do) because of the extreme crisis the world found itself in. A flat-lined birthrate, a climate crisis, a series of natural disasters. In that space, societal need for sweeping change outweighed individual wants.

Perhaps students could present in small groups on their findings, creating a classroom bank of examples when similar conflicts have arisen. Is there consistency to be found between who is right and who is wrong? What, historically has been better? Freedom to, or freedom from?

At the end of the presentations, have students write an impromptu paragraph on which position they would personally prefer *and* which they think would benefit society most. What can they infer about themselves based on their choices?

ACTIVITY SEVEN: THAT COULDN'T HAPPEN NOW, COULD IT?

Maybe none of this is about control. Maybe it really isn't about who can own whom, who can do what to whom and get away with it, even as far as death. Maybe it isn't about who can sit and who has to kneel or stand or lie down, legs spread open. Maybe it's about who can do what to whom and be forgiven for it. Never tell me it amounts to the same thing.[12]

It's perfectly understandable that students will be resistant to the comparison between the fictional Gilead that Atwood presents and the world around us. Drawing hyperbolic comparisons is not useful. However, it is also true that, just as Aunt Lydia suggests, anything can come to feel normal to us.

With that in mind, there are a number of current news stories that have a distinctly Gileadean feel to them. And this is a good moment in the unit to draw attention to troubling situations that may feel "normal" to us, to lawmakers, and to society.

What follows is an article from the summer of 2019 about a case that (for a minute) got quite a lot of publicity. Two women got into a verbal altercation, and then one woman shot the other. The woman who was shot, Marshae Jones, happened to be five months pregnant. The baby was lost due to damage from the gunshot wound. Marshae Jones was charged with the death of her baby. She was charged for killing her baby because she was shot by someone else.

• "Alabama Woman Who Was Shot While Pregnant Is Charged in Fetus's Death" by Sarah Mervosh, *The New York Times*, June 27, 2019[13]

Have the students read the article and annotate it as they go. Again, no matter what they think about what happened, have them examine how *power* is evidencing itself in this story. Who has it, and what are they using it for?

Before students put their annotation aside, have them consider the above from a Gileadean perspective. Then have them share out the significance of the similarities (in Gilead, this would be treated in a similar manner). What does that suggest about the two societies? And why should we care?

This activity layers a contemporary informational text onto our study of a literary text, drawing meaningful connections between the literature and today's world.

SYNTACTICAL OPPRESSION: HOW DOES ATWOOD DEMONSTRATE DENYING PERSONHOOD AND VALUE AND COMPLEXITY BY CHANGING/ EDITING/ABRIDGING LANGUAGE?

This text is, in so many ways, about the power of language in an extremely visceral way. It's about how we take our language for granted, and it's about how we underestimate how changing wording can change intention. The control Atwood demonstrates over the language in the text is pretty mind-boggling. Take, for example, the following paragraph from the opening pages of the novel:

"A chair, a table, a lamp. Above, on the white ceiling, a relief ornament in the shape of a wreath, and in the center of it a blank space, plastered over, like the place in a face where the eye has been taken out. There must have been a chandelier, once. They've removed anything you could tie a rope to."[14]

There is nothing particularly wrong with this setting. And yet, something is uncanny about how this begins. It's sterilized, repressed, lacking. If students were to do a close-read of this opening, they may note the following:

1. Things are gone from the room. An exit has happened, offstage.
2. Things are simultaneously *not* scary, *not* repressive, *weirdly normal*, while being—just slightly—altered. Enough to prohibit choice over what happens in the room.
3. Suicide and danger are not explicit. They too are quiet and polite, but at the same time, always implicitly there in the language.
4. "There must have been" and "eye taken out" is delicate, subtextual language that all suggests alterations, but at the same time, being unsure about what has changed and what hasn't. There is an assumption of knowledge, but no way to be sure. This limbo is perhaps the scariest part of all.

So what is Atwood doing?

• We are constantly aware of things happening in tandem
• This creates a tension for the reader
• The world is both were/are
• Memories of things lost and gone are both then/now

In short, from the outset, there is total control over the language that implies a loss of control for the protagonist. She can't be sure what has changed, but change is present, and it has affected her. She can't speak directly to the alterations, but these alterations have been made to limit what she herself may want to do in the room.

This, of course, leads to the rebellion she discovers carved into the closet. The phrase, "Nolite Te Bastardes Carborundorum" (roughly translated to, "don't let the bastards grind you down") is important because:

• It is a message of hope and strength...
• ...but she can't access the message because it is in Latin.

All of which reinforces the power language has in this world. The message she needs to hear to maintain personhood is out of her power to access. It is the message she needs to survive, and yet it eludes her. Indeed, she has to ask her Commander to translate it for her, thus forcing her to ask her oppressor for help about being oppressed. Language is the answer *and* the problem, there to be explored, yet just out of reach.

Consider the illicit Scrabble games played between Offred and her Commander. The symbolism of the games is obvious: access to language, access to the power of words to conquer another, an opponent. But consider how Atwood uses the Scrabble game also as a game of chess. It isn't about words known, it is about words used, and to what effect. Offred initially loses to the commander so that he'll feel superior, and thus she will perhaps have the opportunity to play again. The words they are playing, like "zygote", are anchored in reproductive terms and suggest that they are playing for who gets to control the language around women and women's bodies.

When Atwood writes about the next generation of Gileadean women not being allowed to read, it's easy to let that detail swim past us, and focus on more important issues. But in this room, in this unbearable present that Offred is forced into, we see the problem of language personified. If language is denied us, if we cannot control our words, we cannot control ourselves. The bastards will, in fact, have ground us down.

ACTIVITY EIGHT: CAN YOU FIND
THE DENIAL OF LANGUAGE?

Whatever is silenced will clamor to be heard, though silently.[15]

In pairs or small groups, have students choose another passage that has this same authorial stamp, one similar to the paragraph describing Offred's room at the Commander's home. They should look for places where the authorial choices are choices of repression and denial, or moments where it is obvious we don't have all the necessary information. What happens to Moira, for instance, or the torture of the Aunts, or the Scrabble game, or certainly the conclusion of Offred's narrative all provide ample opportunity for this.

Give students time to put together about a five-minute lesson on their passage that they can share out to the whole class. These lessons should aim to demonstrate how one carefully chosen passage is indicative of Atwood's craftsmanship that uses what is *missing* on the page as the point of what is *being understood* on the page. Hopefully, students will take the opportunity to see where ambiguity and opaqueness are a distinct authorial choice that weirdly is enhancing the power of the text.

Groups should certainly address the following terms:

- Diction
- Connotation
- Syntax

- Ambiguity
- Imagery

And any other terms applicable to their chosen passage.

This activity introduces a basic tenet of the study of *The Handmaid's Tale*. Who, ultimately, has control of this text? Atwood? Offred? Gilead? Why is language being denied/repressed/exploited? The mini-lessons student groups present are a great way to introduce listening and speaking standards, while also tuning them into larger ideas of craft. We so often think of writing as putting the best we have on the page, but sometimes the highest example of literary craft is what the page leaves unsaid. Give students this venue to explore denial or repression of language in the text, and a chance to explore its suggestiveness.

Atwood is a tricky devil. This is a book about the vulnerability of language, and how easily our very identities are altered based on the language we use to discuss those identities. For instance, Offred had a name and a husband and a daughter before the rise of Gilead. Those most important people knew her by her real given first name, and by titles that made sense to their family: wife, mother, friend, daughter, etc. Atwood writes,

> *My name isn't Offred, I have another name, which nobody uses now because it's forbidden. I tell myself it doesn't matter, your name is like your telephone number, useful only to others; but what I tell myself is wrong, it does matter. I keep the knowledge of this name like something hidden, some treasure I'll come back to dig up, one day. I think of this name as buried. This name has an aura around it, like an amulet, some charm that's survived from an unimaginably distant past. I lie in my single bed at night, with my eyes closed, and the name floats there behind my eyes, not quite within reach, shining in the dark.*[16]

And yet Atwood refuses to let us see this Offred. Rather, Offred always gives her name as it is in Gilead. Unlike so many texts students typically read in a classroom, this is not a novel of *what happened*, but rather, *it did happen, so what now?* Because it begins *In media res* (in the middle of things), we don't get to hope it all works out. The story begins after it has failed to work out.

This omission of Offred's prior identity, one she chose to inhabit, is designed to show the vulnerable ties between our identities and our ability to put a name to what we are. She used to be someone else; Moira's friend, her daughter's mother, Luke's wife. Now, she is merely a reflection of who controls her body and her language, Fred. She is *of Fred*, or, Offred. Her identity has disappeared with her inability to claim the language she wants for herself.

Atwood embodies this oppression in order to demonstrate it. Time and again, Offred refuses to tell the whole story or to put a name to what is happening to her. Throughout the text, Atwood designs Offred to tell part of the story, not focus on the most compelling part. For example, at a horrific Salvaging ceremony, Offred, our first-person narrator says, "I don't want to see it anymore. I look at the grass instead. I describe the rope."

Offred is the only person who can tell us, warn us, about what is going on, but as the novel progresses, her reticence to truly tell the tale increases. It is as if she is willingly leaning into the oppression of language that she knows has denied her her very personhood. She has learned its power, and is now using it against us, her reader. Through this denial, there is control of what the story is and what the story can be.

This is particularly true in the end, when, just as she asserts her autonomy again, and pursues a romantic relationship with Nick, the Commander's driver, she retreats into the narrative sequencing patterns of her own oppressors. She stops telling us what is actually going on. She, too, is working in excerpts and partial truths, just like the partial conveyance of the Book of Genesis chapters that justify the ceremonial rape that happens in Gilead, Offred herself starts offering partial, fragmented stories to explain how she escapes. For instance,

> *I dismiss these uneasy whispers. I talk too much. I tell him things I shouldn't. I tell him about Moira, about Ofglen; not about Luke though. I want to tell him about the woman in my room, the one who was there before me, but I don't. I'm jealous of her. If she's been here before me too, in this bed, I don't want to hear about it.*
>
> *I tell him my real name, and feel that therefore I am known. I act like a dunce. I should know better. I make of him an idol, a cardboard cutout.*
>
> *He on the other hand talks little: no more hedging or jokes. He barely asks questions. He seems indifferent to most of what I have to say, alive only to the possibilities of my body, though he watches me while I'm speaking. He watches my face.*
>
> *Impossible to think that anyone for whom I feel such gratitude could betray me.*[17]

What is Atwood doing? The lesson for students here is fascinating. Her authorial choice is to have her oppressed and denied protagonist take on the language of repression and denial for her audience. If what is happening between Offred and Nick is too private, we don't get to know. If Offred is trying to protect her lover, we don't get to know. Offred's telling of it seems to provide unbelievable cover for Nick—he is, like she is in Gilead, utterly voiceless in the retelling of their final act in the structure of the story.

Does she deny him voice because he is unimportant? Or does she deny him voice because she, then, controls what we, the observing audience, gets to know about her most private conclusion?

And in this way, does the ambiguous ending come to make more sense? Perhaps the infuriating ambiguity is a power play on Offred's part. Obviously, she got out to tell and record the tale. Obviously she wasn't immediately executed. But the way she tells it, the way she crafts her story, is to deny the observer certainty about her or Nick's fate. She, the initially powerless, has ultimate power over what we understand of her and her story. And that power manifests by asserting privacy, not transparency. To play the game is to win the game. Don't let the bastards grind you down.

NEOLOGISMS, MUSINGS, AND SCRABBLE: LANGUAGE IS ACCESS, LANGUAGE IS LACK OF ACCESS

A neologism is a newly coined word or phrase. Gilead uses a lot of neologisms, like "unbaby" and "gender traitor" or "Marthas." All of these serve as a manipulation of language to control the thoughts and actions of those around us.

Give students a chance to work in small groups and create a bank of evidence for how Gilead has shifted language since their takeover. What is the purpose of these shifts? Who or what do they benefit? In contrast, how does Offred's long-form musings counteract or exemplify Gilead's attempts?

Activity Nine: But Do Words Really Matter?

That is what you have to do before you kill, I thought. You have to create an it, where none was before.[18]

Have students read the following article:

- "US Politician Says Pregnant Women Are 'Hosts' Once They Are 'Irresponsible' Enough to Have Sex" by Tom Embury-Dennis, *The Independent*, February 14, 2017[19]

After reading and annotating the following nonfiction piece, have them prepare answers to the following questions:

1. What specific diction is being used by the power structure that is worthy of examination?
2. How are empowered legislators changing language to assert their political agendas?
3. How do these choices in language from politicians reflect choices Atwood explores in *The Handmaid's Tale*?

Students should specifically focus on—and unpack—the politician's use of the word, *host*. This kind of diction repeats again and again in this article, in our world, and in *The Handmaid's Tale*: people in power picking and choosing what language they use to support their own agenda. And through this dishonest appropriation of language, we see how power can be gained by dehumanizing those we wish to have control over.

USING A STUDY GUIDE TO ANCHOR LEARNING THROUGHOUT A UNIT

For really complicated works, consider providing students with study guides at the beginning of units. They can be added onto, but the front-loading of essential topics allows the class to stay focused and for students to see the connections between a six-week unit and a holistic understanding of the text.

A good way to make the study guide matter in your classroom is to (somewhere near the end of your unit) put the students in groups and have them prepare a presentation for one of the subgroups below. They should do outside research in combination with in-class notes, discussions, and nonfiction reading from the course of study itself.

Students who can do this can then, of course, demonstrate mastery of an incredibly complicated subject.

Students can also pair this study guide with their final essay for the unit. They must choose one of the below subgroups to write an essay about, with the same criteria as the group presentation. The caveat would be they cannot write an essay about the same topic they already presented on with their group—no double-dipping. This way, they individually dive deeply into at least two of the below topics, preparing them for a final, allowing them to practice their analysis and informational synthesis, and encouraging useful research strategies.

From this, you can build your final exam in a way that reflects the complex concepts introduced and examined from the study guide. A final assessment could take many different shapes, but consider providing three passages for students to choose from, and have them write an in-class essay about how their chosen passage reflects one of the topics from the study guide.

An assessment such as that will force students to interact with moments from the text and apply concepts learned over the course of an entire unit. This type of assessment relies on authentic learning and application, and will therefore absolutely demonstrate true student learning.

The Handmaid's Tale *Study Guide*

1. The power of language
   a. What happens when you lose it

    b. What happens when you are denied it
    c. As a means of escape
    d. How does Atwood control language in the text? Think of Offred's real name, or Piexto's closing of the text
    e. How does language shape our thought process? Meaning, if "homosexual" or "gay" disappears, and we only have "gender traitor", what is the effect of that?
2. Control of language
    a. Scrabble as control
    b. Reading/finger loss
    c. Neologisms
    d. Nolite te bastardes carborundorum—carved in, untranslatable
3. Abuse of Power—Who does it? Who suffers from it?
    a. Serena Joy
    b. Fred
    c. Offred
    d. Nick
    e. Aunt Lydia
    f. Rita
4. Passivity v. Complicity
    a. The girlfriend of the Nazi in Chapter 24 and her thematic connection to Offred
    b. Ofglen v. Offred
    c. What do you give up when you give in?
5. The Slippery Slope of Censorship
    a. Religious extremism
    b. Feminist extremism
    c. "there's freedom from and freedom to"
    d. Censoring language/thought/sight/sex
6. Ambiguity in the text
    a. Establishes tension
    b. The end and the frustration from Piexoto's lecture
    c. Aborted narrative throughout and at end
    d. Reinforces being in the midst of—in media res, rather than exposition or resolution
    e. Raises the stakes for protagonist's behavior
7. The male eye/structuring narrative
    a. We must remain unsure about the order of this text
    b. We remain clear the last word is one that is patriarchal
    c. Her story, even when established as her story, is not her story

CONCLUSION

The epigraph, with Professor Piexoto, suggests that Offred in some way escaped, and this portion of the novel is so important because it suggests to us that all that we've read is merely a reimagining of Offred's journey based on a number of male professors and researchers generations after the events in the text.

The fact that we discover at the very end—after the end, really, that Offred's testimony is not necessarily as she intended, but is rather mixed up and presented from the point of view of a number of men is infuriating. It begs the question, how do we understand history? And other people's narratives? How could we read this tale about how precarious our situation is in relation to our access to language, and then assume what we have been reading is not likewise tampered with?

This structural rug-pulling is genius on Atwood's part—it changes our perception of everything in the story, particularly the frustrating ending of Offred's narration where she ceases to make much sense. She edits her relationship with Nick, she doesn't tell us what happens after she goes into the van, she ceases to lead us to any understanding.

In short, she begins to embody the world from which she wants to escape. She doesn't have enough words to convey what is happening. She can't even end her own story. We blame her until we realize the order of the story is no longer in her control. Whatever she left us has been moved about to "make more sense" to male researchers.

The final word of the text, then, embodies Atwood's message: language is power. Language is identity. When scholars were separated into "gentlemen" and "girls," power was taken. When questions went unanswered, and injustice went unchallenged, power was taken. When the best students in the room lost their voice, they began to lose their education. When Offred lost her name, she lost her identity. If we lose reading (and critical reading, at that) we lose the ability to know we are being served manipulated, modified truths, designed to control us. Whosoever controls the language controls the person. And silent seething cannot be the answer.

NOTES

1. Margaret Atwood, *The Handmaid's Tale* (New York, NY: Random House Inc, 2017), 271.
2. Atwood, *The Handmaid's Tale*, 33.
3. Atwood, *The Handmaid's Tale*, 174.
4. Atwood, *The Handmaid's Tale*, 57.
5. Atwood, *The Handmaid's Tale*, 25.

6. "Feminism: Definition of Feminism by Oxford Dictionary on Lexico.com Also Meaning of Feminism," Lexico Dictionaries | English (Lexico Dictionaries), accessed July 17, 2020, https://www.lexico.com/en/definition/feminism.

7. Atwood, *The Handmaid's Tale*, 117.

8. Katie McLaughlin, "5 Things Women Couldn't Do in the 1960s," CNN (Cable News Network, August 25, 2014), https://www.cnn.com/2014/08/07/living/sixties -women-5-things/index.html.

9. Denisa R Superville, "Few Women Run the Nation's School Districts. Why?" Education Week, accessed February 20, 2019, https://www.edweek.org/ew/articles/ 2016/11/16/few-women-run-the-nations-school-districts.html.

10. Atwood, *The Handmaid's Tale*, ix.

11. Atwood, *The Handmaid's Tale*, 271.

12. Atwood, *The Handmaid's Tale*, 135.

13. Sarah Mervosh, "Alabama Woman Who Was Shot While Pregnant Is Charged in Fetus's Death," The New York Times (The New York Times, June 27, 2019), https ://www.nytimes.com/2019/06/27/us/pregnant-woman-shot-marshae-jones.html.

14. Atwood, *The Handmaid's Tale*, 7.

15. Atwood, *The Handmaid's Tale*, 153.

16. Atwood, *The Handmaid's Tale*, 84.

17. Atwood, *The Handmaid's Tale*, 270.

18. Atwood, *The Handmaid's Tale*, 193.

19. Tom Embury-Dennis @tomemburyd, "Pregnant Women Are 'Hosts' Once They're 'Irresponsible' Enough to Have Sex, Says Politician," The Independent (Independent Digital News and Media, February 15, 2017), https://www.independent .co.uk/news/world/americas/us-republican-justin-humphrey-oklahoma-abortion-law -sex-planned-parenthood-pro-choice-a7580326.html.

Chapter 8

The Tragedy of Growing Up in *Romeo and Juliet* and *To Kill a Mockingbird*

Harper Lee's *To Kill a Mockingbird* and William Shakespeare's *Romeo and Juliet* are two works that, over time, have become rites of passage for American adolescents. Generations of students have been assigned these books in middle or high school. As a result, many Americans first read *To Kill a Mockingbird* at or near the same age as Jem Finch (twelve years old) and first read *Romeo and Juliet* at or near the same age as Juliet (fourteen years old—Shakespeare tells us Juliet's age, but not Romeo's).

Why are we reading these books? Not that we shouldn't, but why? What is their relevance, and their value, to today's students?

To begin with, both books are *bildungsromans*—coming-of-age stories— and given the ages, aforementioned, that most students first encounter these books, such stories are certainly relevant.

But why *these* bildungsromans? Why are these stories particularly relevant to this moment? Why not simply replace them with something more contemporary? And more accessible?

The Common Core Standards demand the following:

Note on range and content of student reading: To become college and career ready, students must grapple with works of exceptional craft and thought whose range extends across genres, cultures, and centuries. Such works offer profound insights into the human condition and serve as models for students' own thinking and writing. Along with high-quality contemporary works, these texts should be chosen from among seminal U.S. documents, the classics of American literature, and the timeless dramas of Shakespeare. Through wide and deep reading of literature and literary nonfiction of steadily increasing sophistication, students gain a reservoir of literary and cultural knowledge, references,

*and images; the ability to evaluate intricate arguments; and the capacity to
surmount the challenges posed by complex texts.*[1]

Changes to our reading lists should happen often, but such changes should
not be made to avoid "the challenges posed by complex texts." Accessibility
is not achieved simply by choosing easier books; it is achieved through the
planning, scaffolding, delivery, and guidance of the teacher.

Works such as *To Kill a Mockingbird* and *Romeo and Juliet* account for all
of the following elements of Common Core's above "note":

- "exceptional craft and thought whose range extends across genres, cultures,
  and centuries"
- "profound insights into the human condition"
- "models for students' own thinking and writing"
- "a reservoir of literary and cultural knowledge, references, and images"
- "the ability to evaluate intricate arguments"
- "the capacity to surmount the challenges posed by complex texts"

It is interesting that, according to the Common Core, part of a young
adult's education in English Language Arts is to "gain a reservoir of literary
and cultural knowledge, references, and images." As Americans, and, more
broadly, as humans, we have a shared literary history—a shared cultural
memory—and one aspect of an English teacher's job is to foster a student's
entry into that shared experience. And part of that shared experience is the
trial of Tom Robinson, or the image of Juliet leaning over a balcony.

However, when introducing such works of literature to our students, we
should not pretend that the point in time and space from which they are reading is the same point in time and space from which the generation before
them, or the generation before that, read the same works.

In this chapter, we will model strategies for building a unit in which students not only read, discuss, and write about such works critically and rigor-
ously but also, by pairing the literary texts with well-chosen informational
texts, examine those works in the context of today's moment, and perhaps
even question their status as rites of passage.

Which brings us back to an earlier question: why these books? These stories? These bildungsromans? *Romeo and Juliet* and *To Kill a Mockingbird* are
not simply coming-of-age stories. They are stories in which the protagonists'
coming-of-age results from a harsh shift from idealism to cynicism. In both
texts, part of the experience of growing up is watching society fail to measure
up to what it could be, or should be. In both books, tragedy results from the
actions of the adults. And in both books, only the young protagonists are able
to move the society forward.

If that's not relevant to today's students, then nothing is.

TEACHING *ROMEO AND JULIET*

It has always seemed a bit odd that students' initial introduction to Shakespeare is so often *Romeo and Juliet*. It seems so passionate and intense, with the stakes so unbelievably high, and, of course, it's pretty raunchy in parts, too. That said, there is a certain sense to it; just as both Romeo and Juliet are driven by intensity, ennui, and inevitable reckoning, so too are our students.

Teaching the romance and poetry of *Romeo and Juliet* is important, but there is plenty of curriculum available on those topics. Lessons on Shakespearean sonnets and iambic pentameter abound. What we would like to do in this chapter is suggest a new lens through which to introduce and examine the play: what if it is not just about great love and great loss—what if it is about the tragedy and potential danger of growing up?

Consider the exposition: Shakespeare does not begin the play with any main characters; rather, we have a street brawl with characters not seen again in the play. The language is a conflation of sex and violence, as seen here:

SAMPSON *A dog of that house shall move me to stand: I will take the wall of any man or maid of Montague's.*

GREGORY *That shows thee a weak slave; for the weakest goes to the wall.*

SAMPSON *'Tis true; and therefore women, being the weaker vessels, are ever thrust to the wall; therefore I will push Montague's men from the wall, and thrust his maids to the wall.*

GREGORY *The quarrel is between our masters and us their men.*

SAMPSON *'Tis all one, I will show myself a tyrant: when I have fought with the men, I will be cruel with the maids, and cut off their heads.*

GREGORY *The heads of the maids?*

SAMPSON *Ay, the heads of the maids—or their maidenheads; take it in what sense thou wilt.*

GREGORY *They must take it in sense that feel it.*

SAMPSON *Me they shall feel while I am able to stand, and 'tis known I am a pretty piece of flesh.*[2]

My goodness! This can make for an interesting first day of lectures and lessons. The importance here, however, is threefold:

First, notice that Shakespeare does not begin his play with any main players. Rather, we begin with bit players, whose names we will probably not remember. Why? To suggest that the fight between households is ubiquitous.

It spans class, importance, and logic. Never, not once, is the reason for the fight between Capulets and Montagues mentioned. And the pointlessness of all the destruction is, we would argue, the point. We inherit the chaos of our situations. If we are born into the Capulet side of things, we inherit their point of view. Vice versa for the Montagues. What follows is an activity that addresses this first point.

Activity One: Who Teaches Us What to Love and What to Hate?

. . .peace? I hate the word/As I hate hell, all Montagues, and thee.[3]
This is a fun place for a quickwrite activity. Ask your students to write briefly (five to ten minutes) about a point of view, grievance, or expectation they inherited from their family. This is not to say they don't believe in this point of view, but rather this aims to focus them on the idea that there are some things that are rote to us because of where and when we appear in this world—normality in our lives tends to embrace a certain point of view.

Past students have written about gender roles in their households for boys and girls, racial perceptions, distrust of police, devotion to particular sports teams, and more. This is a useful activity to tune students into *inherited bias*. Have a couple of students share out, and facilitate a discussion about where these perceptions come from. Is it easy and natural to personify them themselves, or is this inherited point of view a sticking point in the family?

The second major point in Act I to focus on is the conflation of sex and violence. These are the two sides of the pendulum of passion. Notice how in the very first pages, Shakespeare structures a conversation to revolve around two things that young people are easily enraptured by, and, additionally, that have destructive capability.

And finally, note that these two characters we meet in the opening lines of Act I, Scene 1 are clearly immature blowhards. In the excerpt below, they *sound* like teenage boys in the twenty-first century. This is not a serious conversation; this is a ridiculous conversation, anchored on them one-upping each other with their planned and supposed past conquests. They sound inexperienced, insecure, fascinated by what they say, and also a bit afraid of it. Indeed, when the Capulets walk on stage, it takes three pages of back and forth before anyone actually pursues a fight. Why? The pacing suggests their young age—bravado is not the same as bravery.

ABRAHAM Do you bite your thumb at us, sir?
SAMPSON I do bite my thumb, sir.
ABRAHAM Do you bite your thumb at us, sir?
SAMPSON [aside to GREGORY] Is the law of our side, if I say ay?

GREGORY [aside to SAMSON] No.
SAMPSON —No, sir, I do not bite my thumb at you, sir; but I bite my thumb, sir.
GREGORY Do you quarrel, sir?
ABRAHAM Quarrel sir! No, sir.
SAMPSON But if you do, sir, I am for you; I serve as good a man as you.[4]

Activity Two: Annotating for Inferences

Three civil brawls, bred of an airy word
By thee, old Capulet, and Montague,
Have thrice disturbed the quiet of our streets
And made Verona's ancient citizens
Cast by their grave-beseeming ornaments
To wield old partisans in hands as old,
Cankered with peace, to part your cankered hate.[5]

In small groups, have students do a close-read of Act I, Scene 1 up to this point. Have them focus on the following terms:

- Direct characterization
- Indirect characterization
- Tone
- Conflict
- Subtext
- Exposition
- Theme

Consider assigning one term to one group. Because the scene is so short, students will probably be able to prepare an informal presentation in approximately fifteen minutes. During this activity, students will be negotiating and creating original analysis based on Shakespeare—a major feat, considering they are at the beginning of what may well be their first encounter with a Shakespearean text.

This builds immediate scholarly confidence that this text is for them and accessible to them as well. Additionally, this analysis will hopefully lead them to some truly underappreciated authorial choices:

- The subtext here is that Shakespeare starts his play about the dangers and tragedy of growing up with young people consumed by bravado, violence, and lust—immediately creating a cause-and-effect relationship between their rash behavior and a potentially deadly brawl. Talk about foreshadowing the ultimate conflict!

- Note how the direct characterization does not match the indirect characterization. What people appear to be is not necessarily who they are. Sampson and Gregory's words would suggest they are fearless and can't wait to fight. Yet when the opportunity to quarrel with Capulets arrives, it takes pages of taunting before anyone does anything. Similarly, when we are told Romeo is a dreamy do-nothing later in Act I, that does not jive with the sleep-deprived action hero who pursues Juliet actively straight into her tomb.
- The conflict is about the opaque feud but juxtaposed with the nonsense these young men are spouting, it allows us to infer the feud is parallel to this nothingness. This may be a good place to introduce the idea to your classroom: *Do any of you know anyone who died young for no good reason?*
- If we understand that exposition establishes important information for the rest of the text, it can be no mistake that this exposition has nothing to do with our title characters. That, too, is of symbolic importance. Romeo and Juliet are victims of their time and place—an unhappy circumstance that forced them to behave a certain way.
- Finally, it seems worth mentioning that this is the world that Romeo (a Montague, Benvolio's cousin, Mercutio's friend) is immersed in when we first meet him. A great reference point for when he climbs that orchard wall—ascending to Juliet in her balcony is also ascending toward an adult understanding of love and death. Romeo isn't talking about cutting off the heads of maidens or their maidenheads. He grows past this, quickly, and without his friends noticing.

IT CAN BE DANGEROUS TO BE YOUNG

One of the tropes that get bandied about when discussing *Romeo and Juliet* is the inevitable: they weren't in love, they were just young and stupid.

Though not necessarily a premise we should automatically subscribe to, let's, for argument's sake, adopt that theory. This is a play where everyone dies because some teenagers were young and stupid and confused lust with love.

So what? If you are *confused* about something, it means you cannot tell the difference. They weren't using the wrong words with each other (love, husband, wife, etc.) they were using the language that reflected what they believed to be real. It doesn't matter if we disagree with their belief system— it was their belief system.

The importance here is to recognize one of the least studied aspects of this play: it is dangerous to be young. In fact, it can be mortally dangerous. Young people die, sometimes as a result of being "fortune's fool" and sometimes because their feelings (that are real to them, though seemingly temporary to those observing from the outside) are so overpowering and strong.

Try telling a depressed person they have nothing to feel bad about. Would it work?

Try telling a thwarted young person in love it isn't such a big deal. Would it work?

Try telling a suicidal person they're feeling the wrong thing. Would it work?

No! Of course not. Our emotional realities are two things at once: perhaps completely off-base from reality, and very real to us.

What's fascinating about this play is how Shakespeare tunes into the danger of having very large feelings and reactions *and* having the culture around you tell you that you aren't allowed to feel that way.

There are a lot of bodies on the ground by the end of this play. The butcher's bill includes Tybalt, Mercutio, Romeo, Juliet, and Count Paris. All young. All misinformed. All acting passionately. And all dead.

Activity Three: Tracking Causes of Death in the Young

These violent delights have violent ends
And in their triumph die, like fire and powder
Which, as they kiss, consume.[6]

Figures 8.1, 8.2, and 8.3 present data about the leading causes of death among young people.[7] Not much has changed in the last 400 years, because young people are still dying from preventable causes, just like everyone in *Romeo and Juliet*. Have students work with these data and any other reliable data they can get a hold of. How do these data reflect the deaths in *Romeo and Juliet*?

Consider that the top three causes of death among young people are

1. accidents ("Why the devil came you between us? I was hurt under your arm.")[8]
2. homicide ("Either thou or I or both must go with him.")[9]
3. suicide ("O, happy dagger!")[10]

all of which are represented by this play. If Romeo and Juliet are merely stupid, then why does it matter that they, hundreds of years prior, are behaving similarly to young people today?

What is it, exactly, about being young, that is so dangerous?

These data are important for students to see. There is a reality about being young—the same age of Romeo and Juliet and Tybalt and Mercutio—that

Rates (per 100,000 population) for Homicide, Suicide, and Firearm-Related Deaths of Youth Ages 15-19: 1970-2017

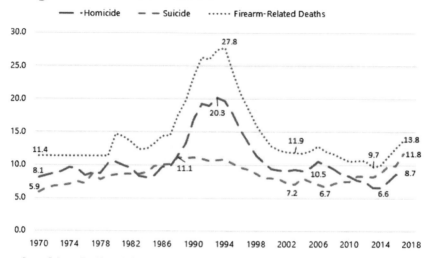

Figure 8.1   Rates for Homicide, Suicide, and Firearm-Related Deaths of Youth Ages Fifteen to Nineteen, by "Teen Homicide, Suicide and Firearm Deaths." Child Trends. Accessed July 17, 2020. https://www.childtrends.org/indicators/teen-homicide-suicide-and-firearm-deaths.

raises the statistical likelihood of an untimely death. Students see this reality around them; many will have dealt with it directly.

What does not often get discussed with students is this: though the passionate feelings (whether romantic or violent) are real, are they worth it?

After students reflect on the above data, perhaps give them time to discuss how those charts resemble their life experiences. Have they buried someone too young? Have they known someone who was caught up in a passionate moment and died because of it?

Then try something a little different. Have students choose either Mercutio or Tybalt, and imagine them ten or fifteen years later. Romeo and Juliet get a

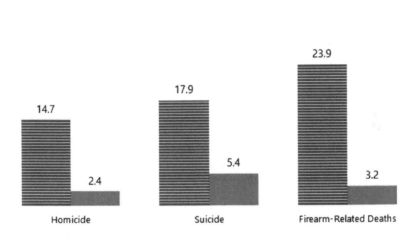

Rates (per 100,000 population) for Homicide, Suicide, and Firearm-Related Deaths of Youth Ages 15-19, by Gender: 2017

≡ Male   ■ Female

23.9

17.9

14.7

5.4

3.2

2.4

Homicide   Suicide   Firearm-Related Deaths

Source: Centers for Disease Control and Prevention. (2017). Web-based Injury Statistics Query and Reporting System (WISQARS) [Data tool]. Retrieved from https://webappa.cdc.gov/sasweb/ncipc/mortrate.html.

childtrends.org

Figure 8.2   Rates for Homicide, Suicide, and Firearm-Related Deaths of Youth Ages Fifteen to Nineteen, by Gender "Teen Homicide, Suicide and Firearm Deaths." Child Trends. Accessed July 17, 2020. https://www.childtrends.org/indicators/teen-homicide-suicide-and-firearm-deaths.

lot of attention when discussing this play, obviously, but Tybalt and Mercutio symbolize the mirror of romantic passion—violent passion. They are also a pair of star-crossed foes, and their impassioned responses get them killed, too. They should be a focal point of this unit of study.

In this activity's scenario, Tybalt is now the head of the Capulet family, perhaps, busy with business deals and endeavors that keep him up late at night. The family is counting on him, and their financial well-being is endangered. Mercutio is married, with young children, but one of them is ill, and he doesn't know if they'll survive. Imagine that Tybalt and Mercutio got to grow up.

Have your students write, from the point of view of their chosen character, what they think of themselves when they look back on the day of

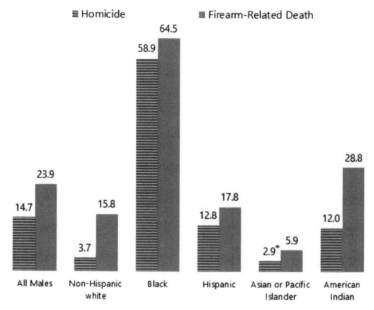

Rates of Homicide (per 100,000 population) and Firearm-Related Deaths Among Males Ages 15-19, by Race and Hispanic Origin: 2017

≣ Homicide   ■ Firearm-Related Death

64.5
58.9
23.9
14.7   15.8
3.7
17.8
12.8
2.9*   5.9
28.8
12.0

All Males   Non-Hispanic   Black   Hispanic   Asian or Pacific   American
              white   Islander   Indian

* Note: These estimates should be treated with caution, as they are based on 20 or fewer deaths and may be unstable.
Source: Centers for Disease Control and Prevention. (2017). Web-based Injury Statistics Query and Reporting System
(WISQARS) [Data tool]. Retrieved from https://webappa.cdc.gov/sasweb/ncipc/mortrate.html

childtrends.org

Figure 8.3   Rates for Homicide, Suicide, and Firearm-Related Deaths Among Males Ages Fifteen to Nineteen, by Race or Hispanic Origin, by"Teen Homicide, Suicide and Firearm Deaths." Child Trends. Accessed July 17, 2020. https://www.childtrends.org/in dicators/teen-homicide-suicide-and-firearm-deaths.

the fight that led (or, in this scenario, could have led) to their deaths. With a sick kid that they adore in the other room, with a giant business deal resting on their shoulders, what do they think about those few determinative moments years ago? Are they still mad? Do they still hate the other person? Or has time completely erased the thing they were willing *that day* to die for?

An activity such as this will help students appreciate both the characterization of these foils and how time (or, lack thereof) works as the most important backdrop for this tragedy. What if Juliet wasn't promised to Paris? If Romeo had time to tell Mercutio of his marriage? If the letter had reached Romeo as planned? Time is the antidote to passion. If we gave these two equally fiery young men time to grow and reflect, would they still look back on that day and consider what was so truly upsetting to them, and still be willing to die for it?

Because Mercutio and Tybalt also live and die in this play, it suggests Shakespeare was not just writing a love story. He was writing a passion play.

Activity Four: The Problem (?) with Passion

But passion lends them power, time means, to meet
Temp'ring extremities with extreme sweet.[11]

Have students write for a moment about the connotation they associate with the word "passion." Some will note that it means you are driven toward something; some will note the erotic undertones; some will merely note it is typically seen as a positive in our world.

Then provide the following definitions. Passion is defined as:

- a strong feeling of enthusiasm or excitement for something or about doing something (according to *Merriam Webster*).[12]
- a strong feeling (such as anger) that causes you to act in a dangerous way.
- a strong sexual or romantic feeling for someone.

Above all else, *Romeo and Juliet* must be taught as a play that both embraces and warns against passion.

Have students choose a character from the text and assign them a timed writing that considers how passion plays a part in that character's arc. Was it freeing? Damning? A release? A restraint? As always, make sure responses are anchored by a clear, concise argument, with plenty of textual evidence.

On a final exam, this topic can be an effective summative question: In your scholarly opinion, is Shakespeare for or against passion in one's life? Are the characters Romeo and Juliet better off with or without it?

Arguably, passion is what killed them, but it also made them truly live. And, as discussed above, it isn't just Romeo and Juliet who love (and mourn) passionately. Mercutio is passionate, so much so that he seems at times unhinged, as in his Queen Mab speech (for instance, Romeo tells him "Peace, peace, Mercutio. Thou speaks't of nothing" when Mercutio gives his speech about dreams and deceptions).[13] Tybalt, too, hates passionately.

And, as aforementioned, the play begins with a conflation of the two definitions of passion: sex and violence, eroticism and vengeance, merged into one. It ends that way, too, with the lovers kissing and dying and embracing in their marriage-bed of death, an image often harkened to throughout the play.

Young people are far more passionate than their older counterparts. Feelings are felt at a greater level. Indeed, according to the BBC's *Science and Nature Homepage*, "Researchers have identified pathways in the brain which light up when teenagers are in love. Falling in love seems to have a similar effect on the brain as using cocaine. It's so pleasurable it's almost like an addiction."[14]

What is the use of that? Evolutionarily? Personally? Interpersonally?

We should ask our students, beyond Romeo and Juliet themselves, are we pro-passion, or con? Does it help more, or hurt more? Are the highs that can be experienced during this age worth the risk of the lows? And are we destined to deal with the fallout of passion during our youth?

IS IT FOOLISHNESS, OR IS THE CLOCK TICKING?

Indeed, first and foremost, the tragedy of *Romeo and Juliet* is not merely that they rush into love. They rush into love because there is a ticking clock established in Act I. Juliet has been promised to Count Paris, and, because of this, doesn't have time to take things slow and make a plan. She needs to take herself off the market entirely if she is to be spared interference from her parents.

And, in one of the most overlooked character motivations in Shakespeare's canon, Lord Capulet states that he likes Romeo, calling him a "virtuous and well-govern'd youth."[15]

This is a significant revelation. Not only is Tybalt's motivation for violence based on a misunderstanding, but so is Juliet's assumption that she needs to hide Romeo from her father.

If you were to ask your students if they had ever experienced or knew of a time when someone was misunderstood or mistook because of limited available information, would they have a story? It is a safe bet they would.

Teenagers love to gossip, and love to assume, and are often on high alert for revealing details about each other. And this means most of them often open their mouths to speak without having all the information at their disposal. Shakespeare knew this—another example of adolescence not changing much over the course of hundreds of years.

Activity Five: Fortune's Fool or Tampered with by Time?

Night's candles are burnt out, and jocund day
Stands tiptoe on the misty mountain tops:
I must be gone and live, or stay and die.[16]

When Romeo laments, "I am fortune's fool,"[17] the English teachers often pause and discuss all the celestial imagery in the play. These star-crossed lovers were, perhaps, fated to love and lose each other. There are often worksheets on the concept of the wheel of fortune during Shakespeare's time.

That's all fine, but for every celestial, star-crossed image, there is an image of time. The "star-cross'd lovers" line, made famous in the Prologue, is butted up against the image of having but "two hours traffic" on the stage to properly tell the story.[18] This demonstrates that Shakespeare, from the Prologue on, wanted to suggest that just as the lovers lacked time to make measured decisions, so the audience will have limited time to observe the tragedy. Time haunts this play in nearly every scene.

We want students to consider how much of what happens to Romeo and Juliet is their own fault (or their own doing) and how much of it is a result of others' meddling?

If Juliet hadn't been promised to another, would she insist on marriage in the morning?

If Tybalt hadn't been embarrassed by Lord Capulet, would he hunt Romeo so enthusiastically?

If Mercutio hadn't been so spurned by Romeo, would he be so willing to prove his loyalty to him in the face of Tybalt's insults?

Assign students to groups, and have each choose a result in the text. Feel free to use the following list, or make your own:

- Juliet's faked death
- Romeo's suicide
- Mercutio's death
- Tybalt's vendetta
- Juliet's actual death
- Romeo and Juliet's secret marriage

Have students (in just one class period) examine the result backward and forward. Their presentation to the class should center on whether or not it is their scholarly opinion that the result—the thing that actually ended up happening—was a result of recklessness or thoughtlessness, or working with limited information.

Whatever the consensus may be, students should be able to recognize the humanity of working with limited information. If we hear something tragic has happened to someone we love, rarely do we ask for proof or data or time before we believe. We believe instantly. We work with flawed information constantly.

Activity Six: The Tragedy of Growing Up

ROMEO Good morrow to you both. What counterfeit did I give you?
MERCUTIO The slip, sir, the slip—can you not conceive?[19]

As we all know, Shakespeare can be a tough sell for some students, at least initially. Perhaps one of the reasons we so often introduce students to Shakespeare by studying *Romeo and Juliet* is, as previously discussed, the passion the two lovers feel is something that often matches the thrall our students find themselves in.

But there is another aspect of this play that absolutely resonates with students and that should perhaps get some more attention during direct instruction: the tragedy of growing out of friendships.

Have students write (perhaps privately—don't necessarily make them turn this one in) about a time they had outgrown a friendship or a relationship, or, perhaps more painful, a time they were outgrown. Not a time when something fell apart because someone was unkind, just a time when what used to make sense didn't make sense anymore to their lives. This is a moment that has resonated in the past for the students; often something like this is happening in real-time, as we study this play. And it's hurtful. It is a real loss.

When first we meet Romeo, he is immersed in his friends. Though he is not present at the Act I, Scene 1 fray, he just misses it (just missing things is what Romeo seems best at, sometimes). We are meant to connect that immature posturing we saw with Samson and Gregory to Romeo. Indeed, Romeo himself, in his first scene with Benvolio, is sad about the off-stage love of Rosaline—specifically, sad she won't sleep with him. He says,

Well, in that hit you miss: she'll not be hit
With Cupid's arrow. She hath Dian's wit,
And, in strong proof of chastity well-armed,
From love's weak childish bow she lives uncharmed.
She will not stay the siege of loving terms,
Nor bide th'encounter of assailing eyes,
Nor ope her lap to saint-seducing gold.
O, she is rich in beauty, only poor
That when she dies, with beauty dies her store.[20]

This speech, with its preoccupation with Rosaline refusing to "ope her lap," correlates Romeo with his young male friends—men preoccupied with sex and conquest—whom we saw embarrassing themselves as the curtain rose.

His next big scene is with his male friends, namely Mercutio, ahead of the Capulet ball. Mercutio is preoccupied with cheering Romeo up and distracting him from his melancholy. Indeed, Mercutio's characterization is anchored by an intimate connection to Romeo. Whether homoerotic or not, it is undeniable that he is devoted to Romeo's happiness. In short, they are the best of friends, and friends are, to young people, of outsized importance.

However, once Romeo and Juliet meet, Romeo begins to leave his child-hood behind, personified when he literally leaves his friends (his childhood and childish understanding of love) and climbs the orchard wall toward Juliet.

The problem is, because of how time haunts the play; he never gets to tell his friends what has happened. He doesn't love his friends any less; it's just that he has matured past his friends being his most important partners. He has met, wooed, and planned to marry Juliet by the next time he sees them. He has, in short, outgrown his friends. And his friends notice, and it doesn't go well. Think of Mercutio teasing the nurse, and Romeo choosing the nurse over Mercutio.

MERCUTIO Romeo, will you come to your father's? We'll to dinner thither.
ROMEO I will follow you.[21]

This is the last thing Romeo says to Mercutio until Mercutio's death scene. This is the motivation behind Mercutio taking on Tybalt in Romeo's defense.

Because Romeo doesn't confide in Mercutio about Juliet and what has happened, Mercutio doesn't understand why he is being dumped. He is hurt and seems to feel abandoned. When he next gets an opportunity to prove his devotion to Romeo by fighting Tybalt, he jumps at the opportunity. He seems manic in his need to re-solidify the friendship. He's been ditched, and it hurts. So he lashes out at Tybalt.

It is worth mentioning briefly that Juliet has a parallel relationship with the Nurse. The Nurse, like Mercutio, uses bawdy humor, and she, too, is devoted to Juliet. When Juliet fights with her father about marrying Paris, she asks the Nurse what, as her closest confidant, she suggests she do. The Nurse says to marry Paris, and abandon Romeo. At that moment, Juliet realizes she can no longer count on the Nurse—that intimate relationship, too, has been outgrown. She lies and says, "thou hast comforted me marvelous much" and never speaks to the Nurse again.[22]

The Nurse's inability to understand her devotion to Romeo (as Mercutio doesn't understand Romeo's sudden devotion to the idea of not killing Capulets) forces a break in the foundational friendship she has.

Have students work with Act III, scene I, in which Mercutio dies for Romeo. They can work in small groups or independently. Act III is the middle of the play, and we have a long walk before the lovers die in each other's arms, and yet this is the moment Shakespeare shifts this romantic comedy into tragedy.

Students should create a thesis statement that answers a very simple question: what is Shakespeare trying to accomplish by the death of Mercutio in this scene? What *does* it accomplish?

This can then transition into an opinion paper, or a research paper, or a class debate—whatever your students need to do. Hopefully, however, it will prove to students that the structure of this play is not merely about young love gone wrong. It's about the tragedy of leaving behind what we could count on in childhood, and about the necessity of, in some way or another, climbing the orchard wall into adulthood.

Answers will hopefully vary. Here are some ideas that have come up in the past:

- Mercutio personifies how dangerous it can be to be young
- Mercutio's death symbolizes the death of hope for Romeo and Juliet
- Mercutio's death symbolizes how miscommunicating in this text leads to tragedy
- Mercutio dies in Act III to teach the audience that the transition from childhood to adulthood is inevitably tragic

Final Assessment

What follows are two possible culminating assessments. These could manifest as timed tests, presentations, papers, or some new combination. The importance is providing students a chance to demonstrate a complex and scholarly understanding of authorial choice and empower them to use their own original analysis to support their ideas. Final assessments that function as regurgitation should be avoided whenever possible.

Option 1: Group Presentation

Instructions: You will prepare a five- to six-minute presentation that teaches the class everything it needs to know about your chosen topic. Use textual evidence and reliable outside research. Incorporate a visual (PowerPoint, Prezi, etc.) to anchor your presentation.

You will be graded on:
  ◦ *Quality of research*
  ◦ *Quality of applicable textual evidence*
  ◦ *Connections and analysis you make between text and research*
  ◦ *Professionalism of your presentation*
  ◦ *Incorporation and application of literary terminology to your analysis*

You may choose from the following list of themes and motifs:
  ◦ *Fate and Fortune*
  ◦ *Time and ticking clocks*

- ○ *Celestial Imagery*
- ○ *Dichotomies in the text (light and dark, death and life, up and down, comedy and tragedy and more)*
- ○ *Poison*
- ○ *The essence of love*
- ○ *Dangers of passion*
- ○ *Gender*
- ○ *The use of comedy within a tragedy*

Option 2: Written Exam

Instructions: Answer the following short-answer questions:

1. *How does Act III, scene I shift Romeo and Juliet from a romantic comedy to a tragedy?*
2. *Perform a close reading of the following passage. Annotate it for literary terms, and write a healthy paragraph about why such authorial choices are present:*

MERCUTIO No? 'Tis not so deep as a well, nor so wide as a church door, but 'tis enough; 'twill serve. Ask for me to-morrow, and you shall find me a grave man: I am peppered, I warrant, for this world. A plague o' both your houses! 'Zounds! A dog, a rat, a mouse, a cat, to scratch a man to death—a braggart, a rogue, a villain that fights by the book of arithmetic. Why the devil came you between us? I was hurt under your arm.
ROMEO I thought all for the best.
MERCUTIO Help me into some house, Benvolio,
    Or I shall faint. A plague o' both your houses!
    They have made worms' meat of me:
I have it, and soundly too. Your houses—[23]

INTERTEXTUALITY BETWEEN *ROMEO AND JULIET* AND *TO KILL A MOCKINGBIRD*

Nearly as ubiquitous in high school syllabi for the past sixty years is Harper Lee's coming-of-age novel, *To Kill a Mockingbird.* Just as *A Raisin in the Sun* and *The Merchant of Venice* initially seem to have very little to do with each other, so too does *Mockingbird* seem a million miles away from *Romeo and Juliet.* And yet both stories are constantly presented to the same age group, year after year, in state after state. Surely there must be some relevant crossover to investigate? What follows is an approach to teaching the two bildungsromans next to each other, in order to draw some (perhaps) underappreciated parallels between the two texts into the light.

TEACHING *TO KILL A MOCKINGBIRD*

This book is one that remains, Gatsby-like, indelible in our classrooms and our American culture. It has not necessarily aged well. The conversations about the limitations of Atticus and the white-savior narrative in the text are absolutely fair and important conversations to have in a classroom.

But one aspect of the text that seems to be often ignored, similar to *Romeo and Juliet*, is the messaging about the tragedy of childhood.

We begin the text with a passage dripping with nostalgia for the days of yore:

> *Maycomb was an old town, but it was a tired old town when I first knew it. In rainy weather the streets turned to red slop; grass grew on the sidewalks, the courthouse sagged in the square. Somehow, it was hotter then: a black dog suffered on a summer's day; bony mules hitched to Hoover carts flicked flies in the sweltering shade of the live oaks on the square. Men's stiff collars wilted by nine in the morning. Ladies bathed before noon, after their three-o'clock naps, and by nightfall were like soft teacakes with frostings of sweat and sweet talcum.*
>
> *People moved slowly then. They ambled across the square, shuffled in and out of the stores around it, took their time about everything. A day was twenty-four hours long but seemed longer. There was no hurry, for there was nowhere to go, nothing to buy and no money to buy it with, nothing to see outside the boundaries of Maycomb County. But it was a time of vague optimism for some of the people: Maycomb County had recently been told that it had nothing to fear but fear itself.*[24]

Activity One: Considering Nostalgia, and How Misleading It Can Be

He said it began the summer Dill came to us, when Dill first gave us the idea of making Boo Radley come out.[25]

Have students perform a close reading of the passage describing Maycomb County, looking for specific authorial choices in diction, connotation, and imagery. Their annotation may look something like the sample in figure 8.4.

Facilitate a discussion that examines the purpose behind establishing this tone in exposition. Review with your students the purpose of exposition (to establish essential information for the remainder of the text—even if the audience doesn't understand what is essential, yet).

So why make Maycomb so boring? Why fill the first fifteen pages with the history of a family we don't know in a community we don't yet care about? Why start a novel at a purposeful screeching halt?

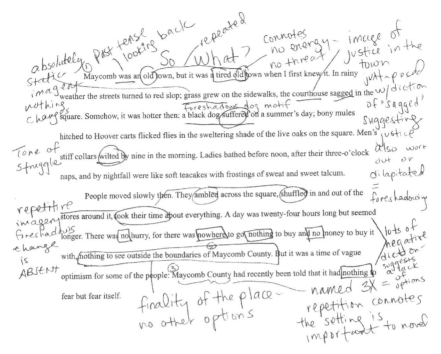

Figure 8.4   Sample Annotation of Lee's Description of Maycomb County. From To Kill a Mockingbird by Harper Lee. Copyright (c) 1960, renewed 1988 by Harper Lee. Used by permission of HarperCollins Publishers.

One theory could be that this opening works well when paralleled with the breakneck pacing we encounter in the rest of the text. Rape allegations, trials, vigilante justice, madmen, monsters prowling in the dark attempted murder behind the schoolhouse. A lot happens in 250 pages, but you'd never expect it after reading the first fifteen.

But perhaps more importantly, the beginning lulls us, like Scout within her own childhood, into a sense of security. She trusts the place she has grown up in, and she trusts the adults around her.

This is, of course, the blessing and the curse of childhood. For children, their normal circumstance, no matter what it is, will feel normal. Our parents, because they are the ones we know, will represent the institution of parenthood. Our communities, churches, and political parties that we are raised with will seem natural to us because we have never known any other. When we are raised with expectations, we naturally come to emulate them, at least for some time, at least in some regard. Jem and Scout belong in Maycomb, participate in Maycomb, and think, indeed, Maycomb is boring. Slow. Aging. Beyond ordinary.

Because of their boredom, they have little else to do but romanticize the little drama they have. And thus, their wild theatricals about Boo Radley come to be. Like all children, they harp on a monster that they relate to as a monster:

"Jem gave a reasonable description of Boo: Boo was about six-and-a-half feet tall, judging from his tracks; he dined on raw squirrels and any cats he could catch, that's why his hands were bloodstained—if you ate an animal raw, you could never wash the blood off."[26]

That is the description a child would give of a monster. And Scout accepts it, and Dill is fascinated by it.

Throughout the course of the novel, however, we get the ol' switcheroo.

Boo is no monster.

Maycomb is.

THE ULTIMATE BILDUNGSROMAN

The thing is we don't get to decide when we grow up. We don't get to decide if we're ready. We don't get to decide what we will be exposed to that will shift us forever away from childhood.

This text begins with three children in the midst of childhood, and, slowly, we see them move from a gothic understanding of monsters (Boo Radley) to an adult understanding that monsters are inescapable, everywhere, and, often, winning.

The Southern Gothic Novel

Teaching regionalism is sometimes difficult. Typically, the definition that works best for students is a story whose time and/or place are necessary for the story to make sense.

For instance, Shakespeare is often so great for theater companies because the universality of the conflict can often transcend time and place. You can take the same script and place it in a new setting, and it works. It reads.

To Kill a Mockingbird is no such text. It relies on a number of specifics. The American South, sixty years after the Civil War, wherein race relations are still dangerous and unfair. That's necessary to the setting. During the depression, when desperate people are more likely to lash out. That part is necessary. And a time in America where children were expected to, more or less, make their own way and come to their own understanding of how the world must work around them. That is necessary, too.

In this way, Lee has given us a prime example of regionalism. Yes, there's dialect and colloquialism and other markers of a particular time and place.

Those help in driving the point home. But the larger idea is the necessity of this time and place to tell this story.

It is also an interesting discussion point when considering the heroics of Atticus Finch as a character. He is a hero in *that* time and place. But as time has marched on, he fails to deliver what would be seen by a contemporary audience as a heroic protagonist.

This text begins with children being enamored with the story of a monster that made sense to them—someone who came out only at night, someone who acted erratically (stabbing fathers in legs with scissors, etc.) and someone who loomed and lurked around town. It sounded like a monster. The first half of the book gives us a childish story from a childish point of view with childish concerns: getting in trouble at school, touching the Radley's front door, and Dill having to leave at the end of summer.

The second half of the text, however, morphs into a much darker (and adult) understanding of heroes and monsters.

When Mayella Ewell says she was raped by Tom Robinson, the real monsters of Maycomb appear. They are the civilized members of Maycomb, Scout's neighbors and school friends, who all of a sudden have nightmarish things to say about Atticus and his defense of Tom Robinson.

This culminates in, first Jem's, and then Scout's, realization that the monsters are the grown-ups they've trusted this entire time.

Over the course of the novel, the children progress from a childlike understanding of the world to an adult understanding of the world. And by the end, the adults have regressed from seeming like grown-ups you can trust to behaving more and more like the children.

It is the adults of Maycomb who demand (implicitly and explicitly) the execution of Tom Robinson. Take, for instance, the following quote, in which Scout overhears her teacher, Miss Gates—a woman who previously discussed the evils of Hitler with her class—discussing the "lesson" she hopes the Tom Robinson case will teach Maycomb's Black community:

> *Well, coming out of the courthouse that night Miss Gates was—she was goin' down the steps in front of us, you musta not seen her—she was talking with Miss Stephanie Crawford. I heard her say it's time somebody taught 'em a lesson, they were gettin' way above themselves, an' the next thing they think they can do is marry us.*[27]

This is Scout's teacher—a hitherto trustworthy, upright citizen. In this moment, Scout realizes the adults she has implicitly and unquestionably trusted to be ethical are by no means living up to her childish trust.

In essence, we begin with a basic idea of a gothic monster—our reclusive Boo Radley. He is the monster of the first half of the book.

As the children age into an adult understanding of the world around them, Boo transforms from the idea of a reclusive, night-prowling monster, and comes to seem more like a man of honor, who simply cannot cope with the monstrous townsfolk.

In true Southern Gothic manner, what began as normal and uncannily familiar to both our protagonist and the reader, turns into the real horror of the novel. So as the children come to an adult understanding of the world, the townsfolk (who are supposed to be the trusted adults) come to mirror the children's behaviors.

They talk about Tom Robinson as if he is entertainment, just as the children talked about Boo Radley in the same manner. The adults try to force an outcome they want with Tom Robinson, just as the children tried to do with Boo Radley. And, after his demise, the adults have a childlike reaction to that tragedy: it fades from their memory. It is a plot that they lose interest in.

The text is structured so that we the audience recognize the tragedy of being disappointed by the adults in our lives. These same people that in the opening of the text we trusted as the grown-ups at the table are behaving like careless children, and there is blood on their hands—and they don't even notice.

The book is an effective tragedy in part because we see how much it costs the children to come to this reckoning. Jem, absolutely convinced that a logical, provable case by Atticus in the court of law would equal justice being done is the last childish thing Jem will ever do. His acknowledgment that it doesn't matter what is right or true in this American court, that an accusation from a white woman against a Black man was the equivalent of a death sentence. This ends his childhood.

For Dill, the loss of childhood is also tied irrevocably to the trial. Consider this passage when he cries at how the prosecuting attorney speaks to Tom Robinson, and Mr. Dolphous Raymond, a social leper in Maycomb, tries to explain to him what is happening:

> *He jerked his head at Dill: "Things haven't caught up with that one's instinct yet. Let him get a little older and he won't get sick and cry. Maybe things'll strike him as being—not quite right, say, but he won't cry, not when he gets a few years on him."*
>
> *"Cry about what, Mr. Raymond?" Dill's maleness was beginning to assert itself.*
>
> *"Cry about the simple hell people give other people—without even thinking. Cry about the hell white people give colored folks, without even stopping to think that they're people, too."*[28]

Dill has an innocent's reaction to what he has witnessed; to cry in the face of injustice is understandable. However, what Mr. Raymond suggests is such innocence cannot possibly last. He will, through repetition, become desensitized to other's injustices. It will come to feel, unbelievably, normal.

This aspect of *Mockingbird* is a rich area to dive into with our students. Sure, it's a solidly good narrative with a distinct, honest, charming narrative voice. But what it really manages, that so few texts do, is to help us learn lessons about our world in tandem with our narrator. Lee, through Scout's voice, returns us to our childhood, and we see again the absolute sin of all the mockingbirds we have, by our silence and complicity, ourselves killed.

Activity Two: Tracking Moments of Bildungsroman throughout the Text

They're ugly, but those are the facts of life.[29]

With these instances in mind, have students write about the moment, in their opinion, that Scout accomplishes her bildungsroman. What happens, and why (and how) does it shift her more toward an adult understanding of the world?

This would make a compelling essay topic, or class presentation, or Socratic Seminar.

If you choose to make it a presentation, consider what each child's descent—or ascent—into adulthood shows us. Why does each of their bildungsroman moments affect the audience? And the text itself?

Activity Three: When It Happened to Us ... Writing Your Own Bildungsroman

"Atticus, he was real nice."
"Most people are, Scout, when you finally see them."[30]

Assign students a personal narrative. However, instead of the cliché task they may be trained to expect, challenge them to write in their own younger voice, and tell the story of the exact moment when something occurred, either concretely or abstractly, that forced them forevermore away from childhood, and into their beginnings of an adult understanding of the world.

Students may write about hearing their parents fight, or not having enough to eat, or overhearing a parent express dismay or disappointment in them. It can be anything (remembering, of course, that we are all mandated reporters), but it has to:

a. Be narrated in the voice of the age they were when it happened
b. Avoid summary and account for the details of the moment. Take us back to that moment.

This assignment will allow students to see that they themselves have suffered these tragedies of growing up. They were monumental to us when they happened, but the world didn't stop turning, and for most of us, no one even knew it had just happened. We just went to sleep unalterably different, unable to ever be a child again. So very necessary, but not without a bit of sadness to the necessity of it.

The maturity and gravity of this portion of the text is something that seems highly under-investigated in a typical classroom. How does Lee, by emulating a child's voice and reaction, come to also implicate her audience to the same misdeeds Scout and her brother fell victim to?

THE OL' SWITCHEROO

We begin with a text that both lulls us into a sense of nostalgia and simultaneously makes us trust where we are and who we are with. Isn't that the great power of Atticus Finch after all these years? He is a person whom we were raised to trust? A person who tried to do the right thing?

This text has endured the test of time for a number of reasons: it's beautifully paced, it's perfectly told, and, most interestingly, it makes us part of the problem. Because we accept the slow, boring description of Maycomb, we fail to recognize the literal danger such a society presents. It is an environment ripe for the killing of mockingbirds, so to speak. And if we let a mockingbird be silenced, even if we didn't do it ourselves, aren't we also guilty?

It was so boring, we didn't recognize the evil of it.

It was so quiet, we didn't know it needed to be stopped.

We, the audience, have a childlike interest in Boo Radley, too. It's our fault, too.

Not bad, right?

And, if you're willing to get really radical, you could consider this same upending strategy as the impetus behind *Go Set a Watchman,* Lee's second novel, which we will discuss at more length below. After America lauded Atticus Finch for generations, after we pointed to him (with, one could say, childlike adoration, just like Scout) as the example of a stand-up citizen, we get a disappointing Atticus, an old man with flaws who simply cannot live up to his daughter's expectations of him.

Activity Four: Idealism versus Cynicism

Scout, I think I'm beginning to understand something. I think I'm beginning to understand why Boo Radley's stayed shut up in the house all this time. It's because he wants to stay inside.[31]

The following are two terms—idealism and cynicism—that students may not be fully familiar with but that will help them to better understand what is happening to the characters in the novel.

- Idealism is the belief that things will happen as they should (according to what is right and what is wrong).
- Cynicism is the knowledge (based on experience) that things often do not happen as they should.

Besides these basic definitions, students should also understand that idealism is often associated with *youth* while cynicism is often associated with *adulthood*.

To demonstrate these opposing forces in the novel, present students with the following scene, from Chapter 21, a moment that comes between Atticus's closing argument and the revelation of the verdict.

> *Atticus and Calpurnia met us downstairs. Calpurnia looked peeved, but Atticus looked exhausted.*
>
> *Jem was jumping in excitement. "We've won, haven't we?"*
>
> *"I've no idea," said Atticus shortly. "You've been here all afternoon? Go home with Calpurnia and get your supper—and stay home."*
>
> *"Aw, Atticus, let us come back," pleaded Jem. "Please let us hear the verdict, please sir."*
>
> *"The jury might be out and back in a minute, we don't know-" but we could tell Atticus was relenting. "Well, you've heard it all, so you might as well hear the rest. Tell you what, you all can come back when you've eaten your supper— eat slowly, now, you won't miss anything important—and if the jury's still out, you can wait with us. But I expect it'll be over before you get back."*
>
> *"You think they'll acquit him that fast?"*
>
> *Atticus opened his mouth to answer, but shut it and left us.*[32]

After reviewing this scene, ask students the following questions:

- In this scene, one character is sure of something, and another character is sure of the opposite.
- What is Jem sure of, and why is he sure of that? What is Atticus sure of, and why is he sure of that?
- Which character is exhibiting idealism, and which character is exhibiting cynicism?

Students will recognize, of course, that Jem's youth allows him to view the world he lives in idealistically—what should happen will happen. Based on the court proceeding, Tom has clearly been proven innocent and, therefore, will be acquitted.

Atticus, however, knows better. Atticus's experiences in that same world tell him—perhaps cynically, but nevertheless true—that while Tom may be innocent of raping Mayella Ewell, he is still guilty of being Black, and the white jury—representing the people of quiet, old Maycomb County, Alabama—will convict Tom of that crime promptly and be home for supper.

It is important to discuss with students the subtext beneath Atticus's answer to Jem's question, "You think they'll acquit him that fast?" Lee chooses to have Atticus answer his son with silence, but, though Jem doesn't know it yet, that silence speaks volumes.

This conversation is echoed when Jem, Scout, and Dill return to the courtroom to hear the verdict, in a conversation between Jem and Reverend Sykes:

> *I thought he was leanin' a little to our side—" Reverend Sykes scratched his head.*
>
> *Jem smiled. "He's not supposed to lean, Reverend, but don't fret, we've won it," he said wisely. "Don't see how any jury can convict on what we heard—"*
>
> *"Now don't be so confident, Mr. Jem, I ain't ever seen any jury decide in favor of a colored man over a white man." But Jem took exception to Reverend Sykes, and we were subjected to a lengthy review of the evidence*[33]

Again, we see the cynicism of the adult character, based on repeated experiences of racial injustice in the court system, juxtaposed with the idealism of the child, who, in this case, confuses naiveté with wisdom.

In the scenes that follow these conversations, we see the process of Jem's coming-of-age brought to completion. And it comes in the form of a harsh shift from idealism to cynicism. In one moment, with one verdict, the world that Jem thought he lived in falls away, and the horror of the world he actually lives in shows itself.

As the verdict is read, Lee uses a simile to demonstrate the pain of that moment: "I shut my eyes. Judge Taylor was polling the jury: 'Guilty . . . guilty . . . guilty . . . guilty. . .' I peeked at Jem: his hands were white from gripping the balcony rail, and his shoulders jerked as if each 'guilty' was a separate stab between them."[34]

Part of this pain, whether Jem understands it or not, is that the adults in his life, and in his community, have failed him, and they have failed Tom Robinson in that they have failed to create a community in which an innocent man—any innocent man—is innocent. The adults have failed to make the world *just*, a truth that Lee reinforces when Aunt Alexandra asks Atticus if the distraught Jem is going to be okay. Atticus responds that "He will be so presently."

When students unpack this response, they will find that what it suggests is not that the world Jem has now entered will improve, but that Jem will come to accept that world and its injustice, just as Atticus has, which is truly sad.

Aunt Alexandra then tells Atticus that she knew it was a bad idea to let the children hear the verdict, to which Atticus gives the following response, which, as mentioned, Lee uses to reinforce the failure of the adults in Jem's life: "This is their home, sister," said Atticus. "We've made it this way for them, they might as well learn to cope with it."[35]

Finally, in Chapter 23, Lee juxtaposes Scout's idealism with Jem's new-found cynicism when Scout says to Jem that "there's just one kind of folks. Folks."

Jem responds:

> *That's what I thought, too, [. . .] when I was your age. If there's just one kind of folks, why can't they get along with each other? If they're all alike, why do they go out of their way to despise each other? Scout, I think I'm beginning to understand something. I think I'm beginning to understand why Boo Radley's stayed shut up in the house all this time . . . it's because he wants to stay inside.*[36]

Here, eight chapters from the novel's end, we see that Jem has become a hardened cynic. But what will happen to Scout's idealism?

TO KILL A MOCKINGBIRD FINAL ESSAY

Once students have finished reading *To Kill a Mockingbird*, they will have participated in an American tradition of reading Lee's novel in middle or high school. For this final essay, they will explore the extent to which their reading of the novel is unique given their particular point in time and space. Based on this exploration, they will evaluate whether or not *To Kill a Mockingbird* should remain a tradition in American schools.

For these purposes, there are three events in the recent history of this novel that students should be made aware of:

1. A Mississippi school board's 2017 decision to ban *To Kill a Mockingbird* from its classrooms (one of the latest in a series of such bans over the past several decades)

2. The 2015 publication of Lee's only other novel, *Go Set a Watchman*
3. Aaron Sorkin's 2018 Broadway adaptation of *To Kill a Mockingbird*

Banning *To Kill a Mockingbird*

The recent removal of the novel from a school district in Mississippi provides an opportunity for students to practice their research and informational reading skills. For example, students can read the following news report, identify and evaluate the reasons for the school board's decision, and cite supporting evidence from the report. The school board decision received a hefty amount of criticism, and students can also identify and evaluate the arguments of the critics.

- "School District Pulls *To Kill a Mockingbird*: 'It Makes People Uncomfortable'" by Daniel Politi, *Slate*, October 4, 2017.[37]

This is yet another example of an opportunity to layer the study of an informational text onto the study of a literary text, thus creating more meaningful connections between literary and informational reading.

Students can also conduct a short research project focused on the history of such challenges to the teaching of *To Kill a Mockingbird* in schools. The following History.com article places the Mississippi decision in the context of similar decisions over the years.

- "Why 'To Kill a Mockingbird' Keeps Getting Banned" by Becky Little, *History Stories,* History.com, October 16, 2017.[38]

Additionally, the following two articles provide opposing views on whether or not *To Kill a Mockingbird* should be taught in schools:

- "Why Are We Still Teaching 'To Kill a Mockingbird' in Schools?" by Alice Randall, *Think: Opinion, Analysis, Essays*, NBCNews.com, October 19, 2017.[39]
- "We Shouldn't Always Feel Comfortable: Why 'To Kill a Mockingbird' Matters" by Christina Torres, *Education Week*, October 15, 2017.[40]

This series of articles provides great fodder for classroom discussion. Students should be writing about and talking about the complex questions brought up in these texts. This can be done informally or formally, such as in a class debate or a Socratic Seminar, all of which will provide a foundation for the final essay.

The Publication of *Go Set a Watchman*[41]

Harper Lee's *To Kill a Mockingbird* was first published in 1960. It won the 1961 Pulitzer Prize and made Lee famous. It still sells thousands of copies every year. Lee never published another book until *Go Set a Watchman* in 2015, seven months before her death.

The protagonist of *Go Set a Watchman* is Scout—Jean Louise Finch—all grown up and returning to Maycomb from New York City. But *Watchman* is not a typical sequel in that, as students will be interested to learn, Lee wrote it first. And then put it aside to write *Mockingbird*.

There are two "controversies" surrounding this second novel (and students love controversies), the first of which is intriguing, but only the second of which is relevant to our students' final essays.

1. If Lee intended to publish *Watchman*, why did she wait fifty years to do so? Given that she was eighty-nine years old, and given the earning potential of a long-awaited *Mockingbird* sequel, was she taken advantage of?
2. The Atticus Finch that Lee depicts in *Watchman* is not the hero of racial justice who was depicted in *Mockingbird* and who Americans have admired for half a century.

The following videos will provide students some context for the second of the above controversies.

- "'Go Set A Watchman' Incites Controversy Over Race"[42]

This clip from a broadcast of the CBS Evening News the night before *Go Set a Watchman* was released describes the early reactions to an Atticus Finch who, in the new book, is "a segregationist, with ties to the KKK." The report also describes Atticus as "a complicated figure, more reflective of the era in which he lived."

- Brown v. Board of Education | BRI's Homework Help Series[43]

In *Go Set a Watchman*, part of the conflict between Jean Louise (the grown-up Scout) and her father stems from Atticus's opinions on the US Supreme Court's 1954 decision in Brown v. Board of Education in Topeka, KS—the case that deemed racially segregated schools to be unconstitutional. It is Atticus's opinions on this case that reveal him, in the new novel, to be a segregationist.

The Brown decision is also referenced in the next video, and students should have a basic knowledge of the case, if they do not already. This four-minute video provides a thorough but accessible overview.

- "How Harper Lee's Alternative Take on Atticus Finch May Resonate with Readers"[44]

This clip from a PBS NewsHour broadcast features a discussion of *Go Set a Watchman*, and its surrounding controversies, with Wayne Flynt, a professor and personal friend of Lee's, and Natasha Trethewey, the former US Poet Laureate. This video is interesting, and helpful to our students' ultimate purpose, as it introduces the concept of *disillusionment*. Both guests describe, as they came of age, a growing disillusionment with their own fathers similar to Lee's disillusionment with her father, Amasa Coleman Lee, who was the prototype for Atticus Finch.

Disillusionment

Students should understand the concept of disillusionment as follows:

- Disillusionment is a feeling of disappointment resulting from the discovery that something is not as good as one believed it to be

In other words, an *illusion* is shattered. This concept, of course, is closely related to the concepts of idealism and cynicism. In what we earlier described as a harsh shift from idealism to cynicism, Jem's coming-of-age as a result of the verdict represents the destruction of an illusion. In this case, that illusion was of a just world.

Ultimately, what we want our students to understand about *Go Set a Watchman* is that it is controversial because millions of readers, for whom reading *To Kill a Mockingbird* was a rite of passage, were suddenly disillusioned by the portrayal of Atticus Finch.

Aaron Sorkin's 2018 Broadway Adaptation

The third and last of our recent developments in the history of *To Kill a Mockingbird* is an adaptation of the novel into a Broadway play. This new version of *Mockingbird* opened on Broadway on December 13, 2018, and is still running.

Like the publication of *Go Set a Watchman*, the Broadway adaptation has met some controversy. The following video clip gives students an overview of Sorkin's adaptation and the controversy surrounding it.

- "How Aaron Sorkin Reworked 'To Kill a Mockingbird' for Broadway"[45]

This clip from a PBS NewsHour broadcast describes the Lee estate's lawsuit against the play's producers (Harper Lee had passed away in 2016). The Lee estate disagreed with changes to the story that included the expansion of the roles of African American characters, specifically Calpurnia and Tom Robinson, and, like in *Go Set a Watchman,* the portrayal of a more morally complex Atticus Finch.

In the video, both Sorkin and the actors in the play discuss the fact that, despite the story's 1930s setting, it is impossible for the play, in the context of 2018, not to differ from the 1960 novel or the 1962 film.

That is an important point for our students to understand and that they should apply to their reading of the novel itself. They are reading a book that generations of students before them have read at the same age, but no other readers read the novel at the same time and in the same place that they did. A book such as *To Kill a Mockingbird*, written sixty years ago, or even a play such as *Romeo and Juliet*, written centuries ago, is alive in that it is inseparable from the specific moment in which a reader picks it up for the first time, or picks it up again.

When a student reads *To Kill a Mockingbird* in 2020, that reading experience is inseparable from Black Lives Matter, Charlottesville, George Floyd. Therefore, they should not be artificially separated in the classroom. A unit on *To Kill a Mockingbird*, a novel set nearly 100 years ago, is the time to discuss 2020. In fact, the novel is the tool with which to talk about 2020.

Therefore, a reflective essay, in which students discuss the experience of reading the novel (and participating in an American tradition) within the context of their point in time and space, seems appropriate.

Final Essay Prompt

The following is an example of a culminating essay prompt that asks students to reflect on the moment in which they participated in the tradition of reading *To Kill a Mockingbird* and to also evaluate whether or not the novel should remain a tradition in American schools.

Like generations of students before you, you have just completed the rite-of-passage of reading To Kill a Mockingbird *in high school; however, you are unique in that no previous readers have shared the exact same time, place, and space as you.*

Write a multi-paragraph argumentative essay in response to the following question: should To Kill a Mockingbird *continue to be taught to high school students? In your response, consider whether or not our point of view of the novel (and its characters) has changed (or should have changed) over time. Specifically, is Harper Lee's depiction of social roles (published in 1960) useful to the education of students today?*

THE WAY FORWARD: FINAL WORDS
ON OUR "SEA OF TROUBLES"

Romeo and Juliet and *To Kill a Mockingbird*: two books that demonstrate the tragedy of growing up in a world that is not as it should be. A world in which the adults have failed to create a world, for their children, that is safe and that is just.

But, two books in which the children, initiated into that world, move it forward.

On the morning of February 14, 2018—for the students of Marjory Stoneman Douglas High School in Parkland, FL—it was just Valentine's Day. By the end of the day, for those who survived, it was a new world. A world in which the adults had failed to keep them safe.

And for several of those surviving students, it was a coming-of-age, and a call to action. They organized. They marched. They changed minds. They changed laws. They are still going, moving their new world forward.

Just over two months later, the Parkland students—specifically Cameron Kasky, Jaclyn Corin, David Hogg, Emma González, and Alex Wind—were featured on the cover of Time Magazine as part of the 2018 Time 100, with an accompanying essay by former president Barack Obama.

President Obama said the following:

America's response to mass shootings has long followed a predictable pattern. We mourn. Offer thoughts and prayers. Speculate about the motives. And then—even as no developed country endures a homicide rate like ours, a difference explained largely by pervasive accessibility to guns; even as the majority of gun owners support commonsense reforms—the political debate spirals into acrimony and paralysis.

This time, something different is happening. This time, our children are calling us to account.

The Parkland, Fla., students don't have the kind of lobbyists or big budgets for attack ads that their opponents do. Most of them can't even vote yet.

But they have the power so often inherent in youth: to see the world anew; to reject the old constraints, outdated conventions and cowardice too often dressed up as wisdom.

The power to insist that America can be better.

Seared by memories of seeing their friends murdered at a place they believed to be safe, these young leaders don't intimidate easily. They see the NRA and its allies—whether mealy-mouthed politicians or mendacious commentators peddling conspiracy theories—as mere shills for those who make money selling weapons of war to whoever can pay. They're as comfortable speaking truth to power as they are dismissive of platitudes and punditry. And they live to mobilize their peers.

Already, they've had some success persuading statehouses and some of the biggest gun retailers to change. Now it gets harder. A Republican Congress remains unmoved. NRA scare tactics still sway much of the country. Progress will be slow and frustrating.

But by bearing witness to carnage, by asking tough questions and demanding real answers, the Parkland students are shaking us out of our complacency. The NRA's favored candidates are starting to fear they might lose. Law-abiding gun owners are starting to speak out. As these young leaders make common cause with African Americans and Latinos—the disproportionate victims of gun violence—and reach voting age, the possibilities of meaningful change will steadily grow.

Our history is defined by the youthful push to make America more just, more compassionate, more equal under the law. This generation—of Parkland, of Dreamers, of Black Lives Matter—embraces that duty. If they make their elders uncomfortable, that's how it should be. Our kids now show us what we've told them America is all about, even if we haven't always believed it ourselves: that our future isn't written for us, but by us.[46]

It's worth repeating: "Our history is defined by the youthful push to make America more just, more compassionate, and more equal under the law."

Romeo and Juliet, through their deaths, ended the feud between their parents. Their tragedy healed the rift that had caused so much violence.

Tom Robinson was dead. Atticus wanted to appeal, but Tom was shot seventeen times in the back, desperately trying to escape a world that he knew would offer him no justice.

But after her brother had been already hardened by the fact of that injustice, Jean Louise Finch looked at the novel's other Other—deemed "Boo" Radley by the society that had decided he was a monster—and called him by his name: Arthur.

And in the novel's final image, she stands on the Other's porch and sees the world—her world—through his eyes.

If Boo Radley is a metaphor for the dehumanizing effects of Otherness, it takes Scout to move it forward.

It is our children who will guide us through the Sea of Troubles. And we have the honor and the duty, as teachers, of preparing them to do so. That is the true work of an educator.

In order to dismantle historically ingrained patterns and systems of oppression and inequality, our students must recognize them.

So the only way to, in good conscience, allow students to meet the Sea of Troubles that they will inevitably inherit, is to show them—to arm them against those systems and those patterns. Perhaps then, they'll have the chance to do better than we've ever done, and write the new book.

NOTES

1. "English Language Arts Standards," English Language Arts Standards | Common Core State Standards Initiative, accessed July 17, 2020, http://www.core standards.org/ELA-Literacy/.

2. William Shakespeare, *Romeo and Juliet*, ed. Gordon McMullan (New York, NY: W.W. Norton & Company, 2017), 5.

3. Shakespeare, *Romeo and Juliet*, 7.

4. Shakespeare, *Romeo and Juliet*, 6.

5. Shakespeare, *Romeo and Juliet*, 7–8.

6. Shakespeare, *Romeo and Juliet*, 48.

7. "Teen Homicide, Suicide and Firearm Deaths," Child Trends, accessed July 17, 2020, https://www.childtrends.org/indicators/teen-homicide-suicide-and-firearm-deaths.

8. Shakespeare, *Romeo and Juliet*, 53.

9. Shakespeare, *Romeo and Juliet*, 53.

10. Shakespeare, *Romeo and Juliet*, 94.

11. Shakespeare, *Romeo and Juliet*, 28.

12. "Passion," Merriam-Webster (Merriam-Webster), accessed July 17, 2020, https://www.merriam-webster.com/dictionary/passion.

13. Shakespeare, *Romeo and Juliet*, 22.

14. "BBC Science | Human Body and Mind | First Love," BBC News (BBC), accessed July 18, 2020, http://www.bbc.co.uk/science/humanbody/mind/articles/emotions/teenagers/love.shtml.

15. Shakespeare, *Romeo and Juliet*, 25.

16. Shakespeare, *Romeo and Juliet*, 66.

17. Shakespeare, *Romeo and Juliet*, 54.

18. Shakespeare, *Romeo and Juliet*, 4.

19. Shakespeare, *Romeo and Juliet*, 40.

20. Shakespeare, *Romeo and Juliet*, 11.

21. Shakespeare, *Romeo and Juliet*, 43.

22. Shakespeare, *Romeo and Juliet*, 12.

23. Shakespeare, *Romeo and Juliet*, 52–3.

24. Harper Lee, *To Kill a Mockingbird* (New York, NY: HarperCollins, 2002), 5.

25. Lee, *To Kill a Mockingbird*, 3.

26. Lee, *To Kill a Mockingbird*, 14.

27. Lee, *To Kill a Mockingbird*, 283.

28. Lee, *To Kill a Mockingbird*, 229.

29. Lee, *To Kill a Mockingbird*, 252.

30. Lee, *To Kill a Mockingbird*, 323.

31. Lee, *To Kill a Mockingbird*, 259.

32. Lee, *To Kill a Mockingbird*, 236.

33. Lee, *To Kill a Mockingbird*, 238.

34. Lee, *To Kill a Mockingbird*, 240.

35. Lee, *To Kill a Mockingbird*, 243.

36. Lee, *To Kill a Mockingbird*, 259.

37. Daniel Politi, "Mississippi School District Pulls To Kill a Mockingbird Because It 'Makes People Uncomfortable,'" Slate Magazine (Slate, October 14, 2017), https://slate.com/news-and-politics/2017/10/mississippi-school-district-pulls -to-kill-a-mockingbird-because-it-makes-people-uncomfortable.html.

38. Becky Little, "Why 'To Kill a Mockingbird' Keeps Getting Banned," History .com (A&E Television Networks, October 16, 2017), https://www.history.com/news /why-to-kill-a-mockingbird-keeps-getting-banned.

39. Alice Randall, "Why Are We Still Teaching 'To Kill a Mockingbird' in Schools?," NBCNews.com (NBCUniversal News Group, October 19, 2017), https:/ /www.nbcnews.com/think/opinion/why-are-we-still-teaching-kill-mockingbird-scho ols-ncna812281.

40. Christina Torres, "We Shouldn't Always Feel Comfortable: Why 'To Kill a Mockingbird' Matters," Education Week—The Intersection: Culture and Race in Schools, accessed October 17, 2017, https://blogs.edweek.org/teachers/intersection -culture-and-race-in-education/2017/10/we-shouldnt-always-feel-comfortable-why-mockingbird-matters.html.

41. Harper Lee, *Go Set a Watchman* (New York, NY, NY: Harper, An Imprint of Harper Collins Publishers, 2016).

42. CBS News, "'Go Set A Watchman' Incites Controversy over Race," CBS News (CBS Interactive, September 22, 2015), https://www.cbsnews.com/video/go-se t-a-watchman-incites-controversy-over-race/.

43. "Homework Help: Study for AP U.S. History and Civics Classes," Bill of Rights Institute, 7CE, https://billofrightsinstitute.org/homework-help/.

44. "How Harper Lee's Alternative Take on Atticus Finch May Resonate with Readers," PBS (Public Broadcasting Service, July 13, 2015), https://www.pbs.org/ newshour/show/harper-lees-alternative-take-atticus-finch-may-resonate-readers.

45. Jeffrey Brown, "How Aaron Sorkin Reworked 'To Kill a Mockingbird' for Broadway," PBS (Public Broadcasting Service, May 9, 2019), https://www.pbs.org/ newshour/show/how-aaron-sorkin-reworked-to-kill-a-mockingbird-for-broadway.

46. Barack Obama, "Cameron Kasky, Jaclyn Corin, David Hogg, Emma González and Alex Wind," Time (Time), accessed July 17, 2020, https://time.com/collection/ most-influential-people-2018/5217568/parkland-students/.

Bibliography

Anderson, Michael. "A Landmark Lesson in Being Black." The New York Times. The New York Times, March 7, 1999. https://www.nytimes.com/1999/03/07/theat er/theater-a-landmark-lesson-in-being-black.html.

Atwood, Margaret. *The Handmaid's Tale*. New York, NY: Random House Inc, 2017.

"BBC Science | Human Body and Mind | First Love." BBC News. BBC, July 18, 2020. http://www.bbc.co.uk/science/humanbody/mind/articles/emotions/teenager s/love.shtml.

Begley, Josh. "Redlining California, 1936–1939." Redlining California. Accessed July 16, 2020. https://joshbegley.com/redlining/.

Bouie, Jamelle. "How We Built the Ghettos." The Daily Beast. The Daily Beast Company, March 13, 2014. https://www.thedailybeast.com/how-we-built-the-ghe ttos.

Brown, Jeffrey. "How Aaron Sorkin Reworked 'To Kill a Mockingbird' for Broadway." PBS. Public Broadcasting Service, May 9, 2019. https://www.pbs.org/ newshour/show/how-aaron-sorkin-reworked-to-kill-a-mockingbird-for-broadway.

Brueck, Hilary. "What Power Does to Your Brain and Your Body." Business Insider. Business Insider, December 15, 2017. https://www.businessinsider.com/what-pow er-does-to-your-brain-and-your-body-2017-12.

Buckley, Chris, and Austin Ramzy. "Facing Criticism Over Muslim Camps, China Says: What's the Problem?" The New York Times. The New York Times, December 9, 2019. https://www.nytimes.com/2019/12/09/world/asia/china-camps -muslims.html.

"Byron De La Beckwith, 80, Dies." The Washington Post. WP Company, January 23, 2001. https://www.washingtonpost.com/archive/local/2001/01/23/byron-de-la -beckwith-80-dies/8f0599c3-f1f2-472d-9b94-960de04197fc/.

CBS News. "'Go Set A Watchman' Incites Controversy over Race." CBS News. CBS Interactive, September 22, 2015. https://www.cbsnews.com/video/go-set-a-w atchman-incites-controversy-over-race/.

Coates, Ta-Nehisi. "The Case for Reparations." The Atlantic. Atlantic Media Company, June 2014. https://www.theatlantic.com/magazine/archive/2014/06/the -case-for-reparations/361631/.

Dewan, Shaila. "Discrimination in Housing Against Nonwhites Persists Quietly, U.S. Study Finds." The New York Times. The New York Times, June 12, 2013. https ://www.nytimes.com/2013/06/12/business/economy/discrimination-in-housing-ag ainst-nonwhites-persists-quietly-us-study-finds.html.

The Editors of Encyclopaedia Britannica. "Stanford Prison Experiment." Encyclopædia Britannica. Encyclopædia Britannica, inc., May 5, 2020. https://www.britannica.co m/event/Stanford-Prison-Experiment.

Embury-Dennis, Tom. "Pregnant Women Are 'Hosts' Once They're 'Irresponsible' Enough to Have Sex, Says Politician." The Independent. Independent Digital News and Media, February 15, 2017. https://www.independent.co.uk/news/world/amer icas/us-republican-justin-humphrey-oklahoma-abortion-law-sex-planned-parentho od-pro-choice-a7580326.html.

"English Language Arts Standards." English Language Arts Standards | Common Core State Standards Initiative. Accessed July 17, 2020. http://www.corestandards. org/ELA-Literacy/.

"Feminism: Definition of Feminism by Oxford Dictionary on Lexico.com Also Meaning of Feminism." Lexico Dictionaries | English. Lexico Dictionaries, July 17, 2020. https://www.lexico.com/en/definition/feminism.

Fest, Joachim. *Hitler*. New York, NY: Houghton Mifflin, 2013.

Fiore, Mark. "One Family's Story of Separation: A Cartoon Account." KQED. Accessed June 26, 2018. https://www.kqed.org/news/11677170/one-familys-story -of-separation-a-cartoon-account.

Firestone, Robert W. "The Simple Truth about Anger." Psychology Today. Sussex Publishers, October 28, 2014. https://www.psychologytoday.com/us/blog/the-h uman-experience/201410/the-simple-truth-about-anger.

Flitter, Emily. "This Is What Racism Sounds Like in the Banking Industry." The New York Times. The New York Times, December 11, 2019. https://www.nytimes.com /2019/12/11/business/jpmorgan-banking-racism.html.

Hansberry, Lorraine. *A Raisin in the Sun*. New York, NY: Vintage Books, 2004.

Hansberry, Lorraine. *To Be Young, Gifted and Black*. New York, NY: Signet NAL, 1979.

"Hansberry v. Lee." Casebriefs Hansberry v Lee Comments. Accessed July 16, 2020. https://www.casebriefs.com/blog/law/civil-procedure/civil-procedure-keyed -to-marcus/establishing-the-structure-and-size-of-the-dispute/hansberry-v-lee-2/.

Harris, Malcolm. "The Psychology of Torture." Aeon. Aeon, July 17, 2020. https://ae on.co/essays/is-it-time-to-stop-doing-any-more-milgram-experiments.

Hendricks, Tyche. "One Migrant Family's Story of Separation at the Border." KQED. Accessed June 26, 2018. https://www.kqed.org/news/11677196/one-migrant-fam ilys-story-of-separation-at-the-border.

"Historian Says Don't 'Sanitize' How Our Government Created Ghettos." NPR. NPR, May 14, 2015. https://www.npr.org/2015/05/14/406699264/historian-says -dont-sanitize-how-our-government-created-the-ghettos.

"Homework Help: Study for AP U.S. History and Civics Classes." Bill of Rights Institute. Accessed July 17, 2020. https://billofrightsinstitute.org/homework-help/.

"How Harper Lee's Alternative Take on Atticus Finch May Resonate with Readers." PBS. Public Broadcasting Service, July 13, 2015. https://www.pbs.org/newshour/s how/harper-lees-alternative-take-atticus-finch-may-resonate-readers.

Kesey, Ken. *One Flew Over the Cuckoo's Nest.* New York, NY: Berkley, an imprint of Penguin Random House LLC, 2016.

Lee, Harper. *To Kill a Mockingbird.* New York, NY: HarperCollins, 2002.

Lee, Harper. *Go Set a Watchman.* New York, NY: Harper, An Imprint of Harper Collins Publishers, 2016.

Little, Becky. "Why 'To Kill a Mockingbird' Keeps Getting Banned." History.com. A&E Television Networks, October 16, 2017. https://www.history.com/news/why -to-kill-a-mockingbird-keeps-getting-banned.

Louis-Jacques, Lyonette. "Lorraine Hansberry: Her Chicago Law Story." The University of Chicago Library News—The University of Chicago Library, March 6, 2013. https://www.lib.uchicago.edu/about/news/lorraine-hansberry-her-chicago -law-story/.

Luhby, Tami. "Chicago: America's Most Segregated City." CNN Money. Cable News Network, January 5, 2016. https://money.cnn.com/2016/01/05/news/ec onomy/chicago-segregated/index.html.

Madrigal, Alexis C. "The Racist Housing Policy That Made Your Neighborhood." The Atlantic. Atlantic Media Company, April 30, 2015. https://www.theatlantic .com/business/archive/2014/05/the-racist-housing-policy-that-made-your-neighb orhood/371439/.

"Mapping Inequality." Digital Scholarship Lab. Accessed July 16, 2020. https://dsl .richmond.edu/panorama/redlining/.

Marlowe, Christopher. *The Jew of Malta.* WW Norton, 2020.

McGhee, Heather C. "Racism Has a Cost for Everyone." TED. Accessed July 16, 2020. https://www.ted.com/talks/heather_c_mcghee_racism_has_a_cost_for_ everyone.

McLaughlin, Katie. "5 Things Women Couldn't Do in the 1960s." CNN. Cable News Network, August 25, 2014. https://www.cnn.com/2014/08/07/living/sixties-wome n-5-things/index.html.

Mervosh, Sarah. "Alabama Woman Who Was Shot While Pregnant Is Charged in Fetus's Death." The New York Times. The New York Times, June 27, 2019. https ://www.nytimes.com/2019/06/27/us/pregnant-woman-shot-marshae-jones.html.

Miller, Arthur. *Death of a Salesman.* Oxford: Oxford University Press, 2019.

Morrison, Toni. *The Origin of Others.* Cambridge, MA: Harvard University Press, 2017.

"New Survey by Claims Conference Finds Significant Lack of Holocaust Knowledge in the United States." Claims Conference. Accessed July 17, 2020. http://www .claimscon.org/study/.

Obama, Barack. "Cameron Kasky, Jaclyn Corin, David Hogg, Emma González and Alex Wind." Time. Time, July 17, 2020. https://time.com/collection/most-influen tial-people-2018/5217568/parkland-students/.

Orwell, George. *Animal Farm*. London: Plume, 2003.

Orwell, George. *Nineteen Eighty-Four: A Novel*. New York, NY: Berkley, 2016.

"Overview of the United States." The Demographic Statistical Atlas of the United States—Statistical Atlas. Accessed July 16, 2020. https://statisticalatlas.com/.

Padfield, Peter. *Himmler: Reichsführer-SS*. London: Thistle Publishing, 2013.

"Passion." Merriam-Webster. Merriam-Webster, July 17, 2020. https://www.merriam-webster.com/dictionary/passion.

Politi, Daniel. "Mississippi School District Pulls To Kill a Mockingbird Because It 'Makes People Uncomfortable.'" Slate Magazine. Slate, October 14, 2017. https://slate.com/news-and-politics/2017/10/mississippi-school-district-pulls-to-kill-a-mockingbird-because-it-makes-people-uncomfortable.html.

Randall, Alice. "Why Are We Still Teaching 'To Kill a Mockingbird' in Schools?" NBCNews.com. NBC Universal News Group, October 19, 2017. https://www.nbcnews.com/think/opinion/why-are-we-still-teaching-kill-mockingbird-schools-ncna812281.

Rothstein, Richard. "From Ferguson to Baltimore: The Fruits of Government-Sponsored Segregation." Economic Policy Institute. Accessed April 29, 2015. https://www.epi.org/blog/from-ferguson-to-baltimore-the-fruits-of-government-sponsored-segregation/.

Semuels, Alana. "Supreme Court vs. Neighborhood Segregation." The Atlantic. Atlantic Media Company, July 13, 2015. https://www.theatlantic.com/business/archive/2015/06/supreme-court-inclusive-communities/396401/.

Seuss, Dr. "The Sneetches." In *The Sneetches and Other Stories*. London: HarperCollins Publishers Children's Books, 2017.

Shakespeare, William. *The Merchant of Venice*. Edited by Alan Durband. Hauppauge, NY: Barron's, 1985.

Shakespeare, William. *Romeo and Juliet*. Edited by Gordon McMullan. New York, NY: W.W. Norton & Company, 2017.

Simons, Marlise, and Hannah Beech. "Aung San Suu Kyi Defends Myanmar Against Rohingya Genocide Accusations." The New York Times. The New York Times, December 11, 2019. https://www.nytimes.com/2019/12/11/world/asia/aung-san-suu-kyi-rohingya-myanmar-genocide-hague.html.

"Socratic Seminars—ReadWriteThink." readwritethink.org. Accessed July 16, 2020. http://www.readwritethink.org/professional-development/strategy-guides/socratic-seminars-30600.html.

Superville, Denisa R. "Few Women Run the Nation's School Districts. Why?" Education Week. Accessed February 20, 2019. https://www.edweek.org/ew/articles/2016/11/16/few-women-run-the-nations-school-districts.html.

Surowiecki, James. "The Widening Racial Wealth Divide." The New Yorker. The New Yorker, July 9, 2019. https://www.newyorker.com/magazine/2016/10/10/the-widening-racial-wealth-divide.

Taney, Roger B. "The Dred Scott Decision: Opinion of Chief Justice Taney." The Library of Congress. Accessed July 16, 2020. https://www.loc.gov/item/17001543/.

"Teen Homicide, Suicide and Firearm Deaths." Child Trends. Accessed July 17, 2020. https://www.childtrends.org/indicators/teen-homicide-suicide-and-firearm-deaths.

Torres, Christina. "We Shouldn't Always Feel Comfortable: Why 'To Kill a Mockingbird' Matters." Education Week—The Intersection: Culture and Race in Schools. Accessed October 17, 2017. https://blogs.edweek.org/teachers/intersection-culture-and-race-in-education/2017/10/we-shouldnt-always-feel-comfortable-why-mockingbird-matters.html.

Wakatsuki Houston, Jeanne, and James D. Houston. *Farewell to Manzanar*. Boston, MA: Houghton Mifflin, 2017.

Wiesel, Elie. *Night*. Translated by Marion Wiesel. New York, NY: Hill and Wang, 2006.

Wiggins, Grant P., and Jay McTighe. *Understanding by Design*. Alexandria, VA: Association for Supervision and Curriculum Development, 2008.

Yeginsu, Ceylan. "Turkey Issues a Warrant for Fethullah Gulen, Cleric Accused in Coup." The New York Times. The New York Times, August 4, 2016. https://www.nytimes.com/2016/08/05/world/europe/turkey-erdogan-fethullah-gulen.html.

Index

Page references for figures are italicized.

About the Authors

Elizabeth James is the coauthor of 2016s *Method to the Madness: A Common Core Guide to Creating Critical Thinkers through the Study of Literature*. She teaches at the high school and college levels and provides professional development for English teachers. She and B. H. James share two wonderful sons.

B. H. James is the author of *Parnucklian for Chocolate* and coauthor of *Method to the Madness: A Common Core Guide to Creating Critical Thinkers through the Study of Literature*. He teaches high school English in Northern California, where he lives with his wife, Elizabeth James, and their two sons.